Now How to Japan

Fresh Discoveries, Further Reflections

Colin Joyce

Sankensha

Copyright © 2016 by Colin Joyce
Published in Japan by Sankensha Ltd.

All rights reserved. No part of this book may be reproduced in any manner whatsoever without written permission, except in the case of brief quotations embodied in critical articles and reviews.

For information:
Sankensha Ltd.
4-27-2 Honkomagome, Bunkyo-ku, Tokyo, 113-0021, Japan
http://www.sankenbook.co.jp

ISBN978-4-908655-01-2 C0082
Printed in Japan

Book Design by Hirohisa Sato
Editorial Assistance by Hiroyuki Morita

Now How to Japan

Fresh Discoveries, Further Reflections

Colin Joyce

CONTENTS

Preface ······ 7

1 **Eternal Mysteries** ······ 11

2 **A Collection of Insights** ······ 15

3 **A Bluffer's Guide to Bluffing** ······ 23

4 **The Demons of Overwork** ······ 32

5 **Last Chance to Tease** ······ 40

6 **How to Speak "Half-Japanese"** ······ 44

7 **Joys of Japanese, Part 2** ······ 53

8 **Embarrassing and Strange Situations Relating to My Life in Japan** ······ 62

9 **Loose Laughter** ······ 74

10　Schoolboy Sentinels ⋯⋯ 79

11　A Tale of Two Activities ⋯⋯ 83

12　Monkey, My Hero ⋯⋯ 94

13　Don't Talk to Me About… ⋯⋯ 101

14　"Lesser-Known" Japan ⋯⋯ 110

15　Strange, Unusual, Rare? ⋯⋯ 127

16　Small Change ⋯⋯ 135

17　What I Thought Then, What I Think Now ⋯⋯ 141

18　I Could Fill a Book with the Things I Didn't Know ⋯⋯ 147

Afterword ⋯⋯ 156

Profile ⋯⋯ 158

A Note on Japanese Words

There are a lot of Japanese words and, indeed, some whole sentences of Japanese in this book. We felt it would be disruptive to the flow of the essays to stop and explain all of these in English. Apologies to anyone who has trouble following the text as a result. We have added explanations for as many as possible on the Sankensha website at **www.sankenbook.co.jp**

We have put names in the English order. Japanese words and sentences are italicised but not words that we felt would be known to Japan residents and people interested in Japan or words that are widely used in English.

Preface

"I wanted to miss Japan."

I have never actually uttered these words but that is the answer I came to when I asked myself the question that everyone asks me. "Why did you leave Japan?"

And people do ask, all the time. They ask me about Japan and I tell them. I tell them about the trips I made, about the fascinating stories I covered as a reporter, about the view over Osaka Bay from my student room in Kobe, about my neighbourhood *shōtengai* in Nagahara, about riding my mountain bike for miles across Tokyo or running along the Sumida River, about the little festivals and the summer fireworks, about shitamachi, the Kamiya Bar, my favourite little izakaya, the sights, sounds, smells, the people! And on I would go.

Naturally enough, they ask: "Sounds like you loved it. Why did you leave?"

And it's hard to explain. I might tell them about the downsides: the lack of park space, the summer heat, the rainy season, the noise pollution and other quality of life issues. Or I tell them about the disillusionment with my job as a Tokyo correspondent, how I felt I was betraying the principles of the trade and letting myself down. Or I say that it was rather that I wanted to do something new in a different country. Sometimes, a bit flippantly, I say that I got tired of bumping my head.

All of those answers are true, more or less, but they don't quite answer it all. Like I said, I wanted to miss Japan.

I was never bored by Japan and was always grateful for the opportunities and wonderful experiences it gave me. It's just that at some point, I began to take it for granted. That was my life and it began to feel routine.

I can almost pinpoint the moment I first felt it, though it is a memory I cannot date accurately. I was on the Keisei Line from Narita heading back towards my little apartment in Ryōgoku from one of my trips to the UK. I was thinking something like that it was still a long way to the apartment, that the weather was a bit grey, that I would probably be jetlagged for a few days, that all the bills would need paying when I got back and other such mundanities. And I realised that something was wrong or that something was missing. I used to feel *excitement* whenever I landed back in Japan.

I wouldn't want to get straight to bed; I would be calling up a friend, keen to go out for a sake and, say, tonkatsu. I wanted to get on the train (the Yamanote!), go somewhere (Shibuya?) and be out there. In Tokyo, Japan! The exotic, exciting city in all its splendour.

I would be looking forward to the coming weeks: places to go, things to do, people to meet. I would have missed it while I was abroad and be happy to be back.

But somewhere along the way, I had come to take it for granted. I knew it was special to me and that my life had been incredibly enriched by living in Japan but I didn't *feel* it the way I used to – and that saddened me.

Moreover, I had stopped making new adventures for myself. I had the eight or ten places I liked to go out in the evening and I kept going to them (they were great). I had the places I liked to travel (again they were great). But I was repeating. I wasn't finding my job such a challenge – a fair portion of it was "recycling" or "repackaging" old stories. And so on. I knew I wasn't putting in the effort necessary to make things fresh and exciting and (what's worse) I didn't think that was going to change, the way things were going.

So, I wanted to miss Japan.

I lived in New York for three years and have been back in England for five years. It seems barely credible to me because my life in Japan seems so recent, so vivid and so important to me. The passage of time hasn't changed that (though I note I no longer know, off the top of my head, the best train route between any two spots in Tokyo like I used to).

I am still largely defined by the fact that I lived in Japan for so many years. My friends ask me, "Any plans to visit Japan soon?" rather than, "What are you up to recently?" Quite a lot of my friends are people who also lived in Japan; whether I met them there or knew them from England first. I particularly enjoy their company as we always have something interesting to talk about. Japan, that is: the places we went, the experiences we had, the funny things that happened and so on.

I have visited Japan on numerous occasions since I left and I tell them about all the new things that I have discovered on those visits, how it has changed (or not changed), about its current affairs and the stories I heard. I also found I remember things that I forgot; as if being away from Japan helped me remember the salient and interesting things because it was not crowded out by masses of recent and irrelevant things.

I got my wish, you see. I really miss it.

1
Eternal Mysteries

Excuse, could I stop you for a moment?

I know you're busy but it shouldn't take long. I'm a reporter from Britain and I wanted to ask a few questions about Japan.

It's not exactly for a story, as such… It's more that I am trying to understand some things.

You see, I think I know Japan pretty well. I lived here for many years and have visited dozens of times. Studied the language, kept my eyes and ears open…

But there's still some stuff I don't get. And I thought perhaps you might help.

Japan has a reputation as a gourmet nation. So why, when I order milk tea, do I get cream in a minuscule plastic container? Doesn't the word "milk" translate as "*gyūnyū*" rather than mean "environmentally-unfriendly, nasty-tasting goo"?

All the samples of foods that you see in front of restaurants… Are they there so that foreigners can just point at what they want? Or do Japanese people start salivating when they look at plastic food?

And which way round does it work? Does the chef have to match the sample-master's quantity and design? Or is the sample tailor-made according to the chef's specifications?

Japan is famous for its presentation of food... which begs the question: is monjayaki *supposed* to look like that? And even if you actually like the taste, is it worth the effort to eat it with that little spatula? And does it really deserve its own street in Tokyo? (Or is that a ghetto intended to "contain" the stuff?)

There are some really nice parks in Tokyo. And (it's not my cup of tea but) there are some great shopping districts. So why do people choose to go to Ikebukuro?

You know when it's one of those bright clear mornings that make you glad to be alive – and on top of that it's the weekend? And then you see people QUEUING to get into a pachinko parlour as soon as it opens... What's with that? Is it a particularly harsh forfeit for some misdeed?

I have spent years trying to learn Japanese. I wondered could you tell me who decided that between the age of 19 and 21 you would be *hatachi*? At what temperature does *mizu* become *yu*? And when rice is in the rice cooker is it *kome* or *gohan*?

What do yaki-imo salesmen do for the other six months of the year? Yes, I heard there was a book but I was hoping for the short answer.

How does everyone live so long? I mean, you do quite

a lot of drinking and smoking.

And why don't women put on weight? I've seen the office ladies at the "*cake viking*" counter.

Why are you so interested in whether we eat nattō? And do you keep trying to make people from Kansai eat it too?

You know how people keep saying "*shikata ga nai*"? Well, it's not always true is it? Just the other day there was a clear case where it was just an excuse for someone to give up and not bother. I explained, "*shikata ga aru*" but people looked at me like I was weird.

Why are you always going "just over there" ("*chotto soko made*")? What's over there that's so interesting?

How do you keep the streets and parks so tidy when I can't even find a bin?

There are countries where people cross the road without worrying about the traffic lights and countries where people wait patiently even if there isn't a car in sight… But why do people in Japan stand waiting for the green light but then decide it's okay to follow me when I make use of a break in the traffic?

I can see you're a bit overwhelmed but I only have a few more.

Who cut off all the cats' tails? Why? And what does he do with them? Ditto for the crusts from convenience store sandwiches?

Why is it *Kuma no Pooh-san* and *Hitsuji no Shaun* but not *Nezumi no Mickey*?

Last question, how comes you are so patient?

2
A Collection of Insights

On a recent visit to Tokyo, I found something while out walking that took me back 20 years. I could have easily missed it; it was just a thin, little piece of plastic on the ground but by some instinct I swooped to pick it up. It bore a slightly scratched picture of two young men in Japanese dress, sitting on a mountain and staring into the distance. I immediately recognised them as Wakanohana and Takanohana – or rather Wakahanada and Takahanada as they would have been then.

But it wasn't seeing those wrestlers from their "Waka-Taka boom" days that took me back in time, though it was rather appropriate. It was the telephone card itself. For the first time in a decade I had added to my neglected but still treasured collection of telephone cards.

My memories of student days in Kobe are intimately tied up with a somewhat furtive hobby. I looked for telephone cards wherever I went; couldn't pass a phone box without peeking to see if one was discarded. I wonder if readers remember that some public telephones in Japan used to have a little container on the side into which used cards could be slipped? Well, you could slide them open. And I did. Often, they yielded nothing but sometimes there was a magical stash of five or six cards.

I liked hotels because quite often people would receive phone cards for attendance at an event, use them to make one (long-distance?) call, and then leave the phone card there. The cards would be almost pristine, with just a single punched hole.

When I briefly interned at Gamba Osaka, my kindly supervisor gave me a stash of UNUSED phone cards that he said he got given in the course of business but didn't need. "Use them to call home," he said. I almost wept with gratitude as not only could I call home but there were some rare treasures. Who today has something bearing the crests of all the pre-J League football teams? The amateurishly drawn little boy of Matsushita Electric FC and the zebra of JR East Furukawa etc.

My "best" place to score cards was Kobe University. I used to study in the library there and, by the phones near the canteen, students would drop used cards into a box. Only later, as I began to read Japanese, did I realise the box said "For Charity". I did my best to pay back for my haul by donating any duplicate or uninteresting cards I collected from across Kobe.

I freely confess that there was something trainspotterish about all this. I devoted time and energy to a hobby that is hard to explain. None of my friends shared my enthusiasm for these colourful little cards. And I don't think it would have appealed to me if I had not been in possession of lots of spare time and very little money. And yet, I collected so many cards that I think it forms a sort of scientific sample of the things that interested Japanese. There was, of course, a bias towards the Kansai region (where I lived) and a strong 1993 bias but I still think my collection yielded many useful insights into Japan and Japanese culture.

I learned that Japanese are not so much fond of animals as they like to look at young animals. It is exceptionally rare to see a grown animal on a phonecard, unless it is tending its young or is one of those creatures that always looks little (a squirrel, for example). Even the occasional grown creature is usually doing something appealing, such as a cat sleeping with its face on an open book. The first lesson: cuteness is crucial in Japan.

Interestingly, Japanese are comparatively little interested in exotic animals. I might have expected cards showing dramatic scenes of whales cresting, or herds of elephants crossing the desert at sunset. Instead, *overwhelmingly* the cards are of kittens and puppies. These outnumber "other" animals, including birds, by a factor of ten to one. I have one pig card, one dolphin and one panda compared to 49 kitten cards. There are slightly more kittens than puppies, but the most popular single breed is the Akita dog. This doesn't, though, indicate a nationalist dimension. I have only one card of a *toki* – the strangely beautiful *Nipponia Nippon* (compared to two of koalas and two of cheetahs).

I learned about the cities of Japan from my haul of souvenir cards and gauged their attractiveness and popularity by how well they were represented. Nagasaki was clearly a star performer. Otaru and Hakodate punched well above their weight. Osaka had little presence for a city of its size.

But telephone cards can be deceptive: you might conclude that the city of Sapporo consists mainly of a clock.

I learned that Japanese love night views (*yakei*) and that my new *furusato* Kobe was rated as one of the three great cities for night views. I learned that many things came in top threes (beautiful gardens, waterfalls, forests…)

Strangely, the many attractions of Kyoto were not reflected in my collection. Did people keep their telephone cards of Ginkaku-ji and Kiyomizu-dera? I only ever found the gaudy Kinkaku-ji and dozens of cards of geisha and maiko strolling.

I struggled to picture Tokyo. If you exclude lone telephone cards, Tokyo seemed to consist of: some high rise buildings in Shinjuku, Eitai Bridge, Tokyo Tower,

Tokyo Station and Ginza. I couldn't see how these knitted together – and indeed they don't really.

New constructions also featured heavily. I found dozens of cards of Seto Ōhashi bridge pictured from many angles. I found plenty of the "far-away" Landmark Tower in Yokohama and the Tokyo Metropolitan Government Building in Shinjuku. Ever since, I have not been surprised when a new monster, however ugly or misconceived, is the subject of national excitement, à la Sky Tree.

Cultural artefacts on cards were relatively rare (though I particularly treasure my simple card of a well-preserved *dōtaku*). Cards bearing adverts for tobacco and coffee are common. If my cards reflect reality then *Izu no Odoriko* is the most popular story in Japan (four cards) with only *Botchan* and *Akō Rōshi* in contention (one each). Chibi Maruko-chan is the most popular character. Mitsuko Mori is Japan's leading celebrity but Shigeo Nagashima appears on a lot of adverts.

Mt Fuji is not just important, it's more important than every other mountain in Japan combined. Indeed, Mt Fuji appears in almost as many phonecards, as every other "nature spot" combined, be they lakes, forests or plains. (Especially if you include its appearances in cards that are labelled "Shinjuku Shintoshin" or "Yokohama".)

Through telephone cards I came across the following

enchanting creatures: the taiko-playing demons of Sadogashima, a tengu (advocating road safety), kappa (two males and a female drinking sake by one of the Fuji lakes) and a cartoon tanuki (carrying a gourd by Lake Biwa). For many years, I assumed all of these were legendary creatures and I nearly jumped out of my skin when I finally saw a living tanuki.

Japanese commemorate some unusual events with telephone cards. I wonder if, in fact, I am the only person to have kept the keepsakes of certain events. Hello participants of the Kakogawa Two Day March of 1992. What were you marching for? Did you march to somewhere from Kakogawa, from somewhere to Kakogawa or just around Kakogawa? What did you gain from the experience, apart from a phonecard?

Mr Kubo, congratulations on your hole-in-one of October 18, 1992! A once in a lifetime achievement, usually, right? But believe it or not, just two months previously in Karuizawa Mr Miyamoto hit two hole-in-ones in the same round. The tenth and thirteenth hole. I must apologise that at first I thought you had made the card to show off. But then I asked my friends and was told that Japanese etiquette means that you had to treat your fellow golf club members. That is why you made the card, right? What a nuisance! I learned a bit about the troublesome nature of Japanese social obligations thanks to you.

Thanks also to you Mr Doi – before I had ever been to Tokyo that card you made taught me that the Ōkuma Memorial Hall is the symbol of Waseda University. How young you look standing in front of it. I guess you made the card for the teachers and relatives without whose support and encouragement... What did you study? I thought you looked like a science student but your "favourite phrase" on the card (*bunsuirei*) was quite literary. Did you go on to great things after university?

I learned that Japanese love trains more than planes and automobiles. Me too, though on my wide travels I have failed to find the steam locomotives that feature rather heavily.

My phonecards complemented my study of Japan. Painstakingly, I at first read hiragana (*fureai*) then katakana (Rainbow Bridge) and graduated onto simpler kanji (Nippon Maru). I learned the names of various prefectures of Japan (and which of them constitute the Kinki region etc.); the locations and nature of various festivals (Nebuta, Tenjin, Onbashira); I learned the 12 animals of the Chinese year. I learned that the orchid is the flower associated with funerals. (I wondered why I had so many cards with this flower and the word "memory".)

But what perusing the cards really did was inspire me to do and to discover: sometimes as soon as I could, but often years later as the chance afforded itself. I read *Botchan* and bathed in Dōgo Onsen. I visited Kenroku-en. Sometimes, I did a thing or went somewhere specifically because I "had the card" (hitch-hiking across the Seto Ōhashi). Other times, I just visited one of the places-people-go and was glad to tick it off my mental list from my phonecard days (crossing the little bridge to the island in Matsushima Bay).

My collection informed my years in Japan, enriched them. I knew what about the decline of the *toki* before I heard Takashi Yoshimatsu's haunting *Threnody to Toki*. Later, I wrote a piece for a British newspaper when the "last *toki*" Kin died in 2003. Another time, I pitched a story about how in Japan you can buy insurance to cover the cost should you have the misfortune to score a hole in one. (I hope you had insurance Mr Miyamoto!)

As I perused my old collection today, I found the magic still works. It's a distillation of many of the obvious and not-so-obvious things to see and do in Japan. Next time, I must see the organ in the chapel of St Luke's Hospital. I really must make it to the Tottori sand dunes, visit Hirosaki in cherry blossom time, meet the monkeys of Mt Takasaki…

3
A Bluffer's Guide to Bluffing

Many years ago, I read a story that amused me. An American specialist in Japanese, who came to Tokyo with the Occupation, had endeavoured to learn difficult kanji and wanted to impress people with this skill. His crowning achievement was that he could write "apple" (*ringo*) in kanji, which many Japanese struggled to do. But there was a twist: barely had he arrived in Japan than the system was reformed (in 1946) and it became standard to write "*ringo*" in kana letters rather kanji characters.

The thing is, I could understand his motivation. I too yearned to have a trick or two that would mark me out as a true expert on Japan. Of course, everyone likes to be admired but somehow my yearning to be seen as a "Japan-hand" was unusually strong: I thought there was something incredibly cool about being seen as someone who had insight into the "mysterious" place and culture that is Japan.

Nor am I alone. Over the years I have observed other Westerners attempting to show off their knowledge of Japan. One Englishman learned the names of every station on the Yamanote Line and could reel them off in the right order – in both directions. (He also claimed to know every line that passed through Shinjuku Station. Impressive but a bit trainspotterish, I thought.

At the risk of blowing my credibility, I am going to reveal some of my "bluffs"; the little nuggets of knowledge that I reel out when I am trying to impress with my deep understanding of Japan.

In honour of my English friend with the Shinjuku obsession, I memorised all the bridges along the Sumida River from Kototoi Bridge down to Tokyo Bay. "The most attractive is Kiyosu Bridge, in my opinion," I would say, "but Eitai Bridge looks nicer at night when it is lit up". I could throw in a few facts about some of the bridges: Kachidoki means "shout of joy", as it was named in celebration of the Japanese victory in the Russo-Japanese War; or Ryōgoku Bridge has been built and rebuilt many times and appears in a lot of woodblock prints, in its various forms.

I eschewed anything technical to avoid looking nerdy. ("Eh? I have no idea if it's a suspension bridge. What would one look like?") The point was to appear to have absorbed the knowledge in a natural manner rather than by swotting, so I would be sure to slip in that I had just picked up most of this knowledge during my walks and runs along the river.

I would vary the "depth" of my information depending

on who I was talking to. Put simply, foreigners new to Japan are the easiest to impress but you have to grab their attention by giving broad insights rather than specifics. They wouldn't, for example, be likely to be interested in hearing you list the "eleven main types of pottery" in Japan. You would be better of just implying you are seeing things at a level deeper than others. You could, for example, mention at the sumo that "this is where the bouts are really won and lost" as the wrestlers face off and throw their salt around.

I knew I needed better material to impress Japanese, but to get some initial kudos I didn't need to be brilliant. A lot of the time Japanese are impressed if a foreigner simply knows something that is fairly common knowledge in Japan. For example, I could just say that I had visited Kansai and found the people of Osaka to be rather "earthy" and a bit more money-oriented than other Japanese. And then I would say: "Kyoto people were different. They were polite but I got the feeling they weren't always sincere; as if there was a lot of *honne-tatemae*…"

I found I could get praise for knowing relatively obvious things: "sake is brewed, not fermented like wine, so it's a misnomer to call it 'rice wine'" or "Aomori has the best apples" or "Kobe beef is great but Matsusaka is actually a little bit more exclusive". Occasionally, I would throw in something a bit contrarian, to imply that I *wasn't* just repeating the standard wisdom. "You know, I actually prefer *ginjō-shu* to *daiginjō*. I just think it retains a bit more of the character of the rice…"

It pays to listen to what people say because they often feed you the lines you only need to parrot to others. Tea ceremony admirers will always tell you that "every movement has meaning". You only need to say that to anyone else to give them the sense that you have a grasp of this esoteric ritual.

Anything that gets you bogged down in detail was tiresome to me. I couldn't name the 23 wards of Tokyo, I can't remember the order in which Japanese prefectures are listed "from top to bottom" and I can't remember the names of the permitted throws in sumo. But it did help to learn a few distinctions. I would tell foreigners, "No one here says 'geisha' – It's '*geiko*'." To Japanese I might mention that I had seen some lovely maiko on my last visit to Kyoto, and add casually "from the Ponto-chō, I think".

My inclination was towards facts about Japan's history and culture. The point was to be able to drop them casually into conversation at an appropriate moment. If, for example, I was with a friend at Sensō-ji in Asakusa I would point out how neatly we can see the dual nature of Japanese religion with the temple and shrine side-by-side.

"It was the norm for Shinto and Buddhism to co-exist this way, of course, until the Meiji era," I might explain. Or I might pretend I was searching the extensive banks of my memory for the technical term: "There's a word for it. Errr, *shin*-something, errr, *shinbutsu shūgō*!"

At almost any shrine, or at any matsuri, I might tell how for a brief time at the start of the Meiji era, people across Japan were gripped by a sort of religious fervour. They gathered to dance and chant "*ee janaika*", apparently in the belief that amulets were raining down from heaven. "Clearly it was connected to the political and social upheaval of the time," I add sagely.

If eating *unagi* (eel), I might point out how it's prepared differently in Kansai and Kanto. In Kanto, they cut it open along its back but in Kansai it's cut along the belly. It particularly impresses non-Japanese when they hear the reason; that the samurai of the military stronghold that was Tokyo did not like to be reminded of hara-kiri in any way. To a Japanese person, I might say: "Of course they could have just chosen not to eat *unagi* but it's a very good food for stamina and warriors would have been drawn to it. Especially in the hot summer months."

If I were in Shinjuku and I caught someone staring up at the skyscrapers and the Metropolitan Government Building, I would shake my head and say: "It's incredible to think that this wasn't even part of the city until 1920. The Tochō outside the historic city!"

At Shibuya crossing I would similarly marvel that "as recently as the 1930s Shibuya was described as an up-and-coming suburb".

At Tsukishima, I would explain: "It got its name because people used to come here for moon-viewing." Then add mystically, "It's strange because, even before I knew that, I always thought the moon loomed large here."

When riding the Yamanote Line, somewhere around the Tamachi-Shinagawa stretch, I would look out the window and point out that "all this is reclaimed land" and say, "You should see all the old pictures showing the trains chugging along the coast!"

If I happen to get off the train at Shinagawa, or be in the area for whatever reason, I point up the hill and mention that the first British "embassy" in Tokyo was based at a temple up there. "Yes, temples were sometimes used in such ways in those days." The embassy at Tōzen-ji was attacked by malcontent samurai twice. "Everyone talks about the Namamugi Incident but to my mind the premeditated attacks on the appointed representatives of the British government were worse in a way," I would opine.

(See what I did there? I implied that Namamugi was

"common knowledge" and I am a level above that.)

Obviously, a lot of my best facts were about Tokyo. But I could throw in some of the standard stuff about certain other parts of Japan. Kyoto's too hot in summer, the surrounding hills trap the heat in. It's very different in Hokkaido – no bamboo, for one thing. Tōhoku dialect is the hardest to understand; they even say that people in Aomori speak funny because it's so cold that they evolved a way of speaking that doesn't open the mouth as much. ("That's a myth, though," I would add.)

I would have loved to win plaudits by speaking Japanese with stunning fluency. I dreamed I would talk in full sentences, with flawless pronunciation and admirable economy of words. But alas that is beyond my talents. So I searched for shortcuts.

Japanese people would be astounded if I could say some tongue-twisters, I assumed. (*Tokyo tokkyo kyokakyoku / basu gasu bakuhatsu…*) But somehow this seemed to get sidetracked into a conversation about tongue-twisters in English, thwarting my purpose. Sometimes, people were surprised to find that tongue-twisters existed in other languages.

I thought I might impress by learning some phrases and expressions but it was agony waiting for an appropriate moment to use them. And then I spoiled it by just remembering the gist, not the proper wording ("*hitotsu no seki de futatsu no tori*") or even just getting it wrong ("*hatarakanai saru wa mono taberarenai hazu*").

Eventually, I did find a few short cuts. People don't take much notice if I know that a person from Kobe is a *Kobekko* but they are mildly impressed if I know that a person from Tokyo is an *Edokko*. (I can top this by explaining this really applies "only if the family has been in Tokyo for three generations".) But it seems to really wow people if I know that an Osakan is a *Naniwakko* and a native of Hokkaido is a *Dosanko* (and, yes, I do know how those names derive but would only say if asked.)

Admittedly, some of my interests are obscure. I have something of an obsession with the Ryōunkaku ("or the Asakusa Jūnikai as it was more widely known"). I can tell you it had Japan's first electric elevator; that it was a true landmark in its day; how it was damaged terribly by the Tokyo earthquake and its unstable remains blown up soon after. It was designed by a Briton named Burton ("a childhood friend of Conan Doyle") who loved Japan but was actually a waterworks engineer not an architect. "That's why the building resembled a water tower," I say.

I attend the Oeshiki at Ikegami Honmon-ji whenever I can. It's one of the most impressive events in Japan. "Not to be confused with a matsuri, of course. They're Shinto

3 A Bluffer's Guide to Bluffing

for a start and this is Buddhist. And it's not a celebration but to commemorate the death of the saint Nichiren," I tell any foreign friends.

If I am with a Japanese friend, I instead point out how the grand set of steps up to the temple contains a paradox. The steps at the bottom are quite high, but near the top they are smaller. Obviously, they could have made it easy all the way so it must be intentional. I invite them to hazard a guess as to why.

It's so that pilgrims are rewarded with an easier climb as they progress, I explain, but also it may have a military purpose. Temples would be held in defence in times of strife. The tapering-off of the steps creates an optical illusion for any troops attempting to storm up; perspective will make the climb look further and their assumptions from looking at the bottom steps will make them think it will be harder than in reality. A small but important psychological advantage to the defenders. "Japan was a warring country for a long period and developed lots of such clever trickery," I add.

Go on, admit it, you're impressed.

4
The Demons of Overwork

One evening, not so very long ago, I was accosted by two men in an izakaya who threatened to carry me off to the mountains.

They were exceptionally ugly (one of them had a bright red face and the other a blue face). They were dressed primitively, spoke roughly and – if you can believe such a thing – one of them was carrying what appeared to be a huge knife. In retrospect, I should have been more wary when they began to ask me questions.

They started, as people often do, by asking me whether I understood their words. I was pleased to say that I did (especially as I was in Tōhoku where I had occasionally been unable to understand people).

Then they asked me whether there were any lazy people in my group. Funnily enough, it's a subject I am greatly interested in and I have thought about a lot during my adult life. So I relished the chance to discuss the subject. "In a sense, I am a quite lazy person. Sort of proud of it," I began.

Before I had got very far, the red-faced man interrupted to explain that in that case he was going to abduct me to the mountains.

I thought about it briefly and decided that he wasn't the type to listen carefully to my explanation. "Hmm, actually we are here to discuss a work project that we intend to carry out with great diligence," I said. "It's a promise," I added.

This seemed to appease them as they then, rather strangely, offered to pose for a photograph with me before going on to threaten other customers.

Eventually it was explained to me that this was something of a tradition in Akita and that my new acquaintances, the Namahage brothers, sometimes turn up to threaten people (usually children) with abduction – unless they work hard.

Cultures all over the world use cunning methods to control and shape their children. In Britain we have the threat that Father Christmas will withhold presents from them. Despite his jocular appearance he has a sinister side to his character in that he somehow KNOWS who has been naughty and will disdain them. Personally, I am not sure this is effective anymore because kids today are able to observe that Christmas is now ALWAYS an orgy of gift-giving with no discernible discrimination against errant children.

I have an American friend of Mexican ancestry who has a delightful but rather unruly daughter. She was unresponsive to almost all parental discipline (especially around the age of three) except when she was reminded of a scary song in Spanish about three witches who carry off naughty children. When she was stamping on the floor in a tantrum, the only thing that could silence her were the words: "Oh no! The witches…"

But even here the threat was to *naughty* children, which is significantly different from the Namahage's interest in *lazy* children. I realise that the Namahage are an Akita thing but it chimes with my belief that Japanese society has a particular obsession with hard work.

In my view, one of the most profound culture clashes in the modern world is between those who think hard work, per se, is a virtue and those who don't. I fall into the latter category and Japan (on the whole) lives firmly in the former.

In Japan, I very rarely hear anyone say they like their work and yet people seem to take a sort of perverse pride in being subject to long hours. Beneath the complaints I detect a sense that people see it as some sort of endurance test they are passing, or perhaps a vindication that they are needed. In Britain, you are far more likely to hear people say they love their jobs, just wish they had shorter hours.

Some of my most jarring moments of culture shock in Japan came when discussing working hours. In my first year in Japan I met a young man who had been given the "honour" of being assistant/secretary to his company president. But his fiancée had broken off their engagement after months of having barely seen him. He apparently returned home after midnight every night and was constantly called to work on weekends. "So quit," I and my English friends advised. "Definitely quit!" we argued when we heard that he wasn't paid overtime, or a salary significantly higher than colleagues his age.

Years later, there was a national debate over whether to move certain national holidays to the nearest Monday, to create three-day weekends. I found it hard to believe there was even a debate: What could be the possible argument against the chance of a proper break? And yet I remember being told by a provincial salaryman that he was opposed. "It's nice to have two days off but after three days you get out of the routine of work," he said.

I was even more stunned when I heard that the argument for the three-day weekend was not so much "you get time off in a nice chunk" but rather "people might spend more money, thereby stimulating the economy if we do it this way". In other words, it couldn't be presented as a chance to relax a bit.

I remembered that during my studies of the Japanese language I came across an interesting passage about a mysterious Japanese illness called "*gogatsu-byō*". This illness, apparently, is caused when Japanese people are allowed several days off in succession during Golden Week.

We also learned to use the phrase "*wake ni ikanai*" which appeared in the sentence "*yasumu wake ni ikanai*", which a man with a nasty cold said to his wife. We understood the sentence construction but had to have it explained why a sick man felt pressured to go to work – so as not to inconvenience colleagues.

(My experience was the exact opposite: I once formed a strong dislike of a colleague who kept coming into work with a deep wracking cough. "Totally irresponsible. What if we all catch it off him? Really distracting... He would have been better weeks ago if he had just taken a few days off when he first got it.")

When I was a student "energy drinks" were not particularly popular in Britain. So I was curious about these expensive little potions when I saw them advertised in Japan. I distrusted them as they seemed to be, essentially, industrial strength caffeine with a few other things thrown in. But it was explained to me that people used them in extremis, to enable them to stay awake at the desk and survive work crises.

By the mid-90s these had arrived in the UK. It took me

a little while to put my finger on what the difference was: In Britain, they are used primarily by party goers who don't want to conk out at a rave at 3am. People wanted energy to party, rather than work. (I am horrified to report that "caffeine plus vodka" drinks are very popular with British youngsters at weekends.)

Akita is among the poorer regions of Japan and one of the most rural. It is not therefore altogether surprising that the Namahage come from there: poor people cannot afford to be slack and agricultural societies cannot afford unproductive members.

If I had had the chance to talk it through with my Namahage friends I would have liked to explain to them that these were different days; that they are a nice tradition but that Japan today isn't an agricultural economy. It is clearly one of the most industrialised nations on earth. (The Japanese "*inaka*" is not very rural at all for the most part.)

I would argue the case for a kind of ruthless rationalism instead. I would argue the value of productivity over hard slog; the ascendancy of ideas in the modern world.

I would tell them about some of the stories that have informed me over the years. I am sure there's a moral to the story that Churchill often stayed in bed till noon (working) whereas Hitler exhausted himself trying to manage every detail and messed up war production by refusing to delegate to underlings who knew better.

I remember the stories I read in Dale Carnegie: of the salesman who realised that any customer who didn't buy after his second visit was not worth a third or fourth visit, even if they seemed interested. He made fewer sales calls and sold more thereafter. Or of the troubled construction firm that was turned around by giving the labourers a 10 minute break every hour. Turns out they were flagging by early afternoon because they were just exhausted.

I only wish that I had applied this kind of logic more carefully in my own work. Personally, I think there have been more times I have missed opportunities because I was too busy and tired to take on promising projects than times I have found that working away at apparently thankless and meaningless work led to new opportunities.

I have heard people in Japan bemoan that "the problem with Japan today" is that young Japanese don't have a work ethic. But I think if you asked 100 economists to each list five causes of Japan's economic malaise, I doubt that "laziness" would be cited once.

As my history tutor at Oxford said of Stalinist Russia's acclamation of Stakhanov and his fellow "heroes of socialist labour": "There's obviously something wrong with an economic model that relies on just exhorting people to work harder."

He didn't mean that an economy doesn't need workers to work, rather that people will work harder when their work is properly incentivised – and that just telling them to work harder shows a wider failure.

I am not actually saying that I am against working hard in all circumstances. I just want to know what's in it for me, don't want to burn out and don't want to work extra hours for little return. (I also want to know when it will calm down and I can enjoy the fruits of any exertions.)

I realise of course that many workers don't have a choice with long hours. I am not mocking them when I write this; rather trying to do my little bit to turn the tide against the cult of overwork.

On my trip to Akita I ended up buying a wooden mask of a Namahage. It hangs on the wall at the top of my stairs. (I like to think that I have "kidnapped" him away as a punishment for his irrational endorsement of overwork.) I look at him as I head up to bed and whisper little admonitions to him: "Don't do today what you can put off till tomorrow because the need to do it may disappear in the meantime"; or "If you have three days to deadline wait two days, then you will do the work in one day rather than three" and so on.

5
Last Chance to Tease

There is little doubt that one of the biggest changes to Japan in the last ten years has been the influx of tourists. Whereas once Japan was a distant, almost mythical land to Westerners, it has increasingly become one of the places people can and do travel to. The thriving tourist industry is a bright spot in the general economic malaise and it seems that Japan is set to achieve its goal of 20 million visitors a year by 2020.

I know Japanese people see this as a great opportunity to showcase their wonderful culture to the world. Personally, I cannot help but see it is as a historic last chance to play a massive practical joke. Still today, Japan is a little understood nation but within another decade it is likely that first-hand experience, or at least a reasonable knowledge of Japan, will be widespread. The world is becoming a smaller, more interlinked and… less amusing place.

Our unnamed foreigner will probably be interested in visiting a park or two: Shinjuku Gyoen or Hama Rikyū, he is thinking. Tell him that's all very well but that there are lot of hidden gems, local parks of real character such as the one in Shinagawa 2-chōme. When he complains that it was just a few square meters of dirt with a single swing, a semi-exposed toilet, a bench where taxi drivers sit and smoke through their breaks and a noisy, great big expressway directly overhead... say, "Admittedly it's nicer in spring."

Doubtless, he will express an intention to visit the "scramble crossing" at Shibuya where (inevitably) he plans to get a picture of himself standing still at the centre as hundreds rush past him.

Tell him that "since it's such a great opportunity" it's not far from there to Yōga: "the greatest interchange in all Japan". But *don't* encourage him to try a similar photo.

If he asks how to get somewhere in Tokyo, try to design a route that involves him taking the Tokyo Rinkai Shinkōtsū Rinkai Line. Make him learn the Japanese expression *"Tōkyō Rinkai Shinkōtsū Rinkai-sen wa dochira desuka?"*

Warn him not to make the "classic mistake" of confusing this with the Tokyo Rinkai Kōsoku Tetsudō Rinkai Line.

If he comes back grumbling about the "Yurikamome Line" sneer that this nickname is "just for kids".

Tell him that to show due respect for people he should add *–san* to their names. Tell him that Japanese sometimes even do this for companies (Sony-*san*), job titles (*haisha-san*) and shops (*yaoya-san*).

Tell him it's always safer to err on the side of politeness.

Then send him off to find the local "*Matsuya-san gyūdonya-san*" and to look out for the cute waitress-*san*.

Explain how you add "*o-*" or "*go-*" to the certain nouns to be polite: *o-mizu*, *o-kutsushita* and *go-shinbun*…

Tell him this can also be applied to certain places of great historical character: *o*-Kyoto, *o*-Ōokayama in Tokyo, and *o*-Nara.

Remind him that some of Japan's best museums are small: the Meguro Parasitological Museum, the Sumo Museum at Ryōgoku, the Button Museum by the Sumida…

Encourage him to "think Japanese". For example, explain that when he eats rice he should finish every last grain in honour of the 88 tasks the farmer performed to produce it. "This is why we Japanese bow before eating…"

Similarly, when he turns on a piece of electrical equipment a moment of reverence is appropriate for the 99 salarymen who rose before dawn and rode packed commuter trains day after day to offices and factories where they imagined, designed, manufactured, marketed and shipped their products. "Remember their sacrifice next time you blame your camera for a lousy picture."

Encourage him to watch *Massan*, especially the "core" 14 episodes when Ellie attempts to cook Japanese food to the satisfaction of her Japanese in-laws.

If he says he is bored, explain that there is a lot going on beneath the surface.

If he is still unconvinced, fix him a powerful stare and assure him, "Grasp this and you have the Japanese soul."

Feign ignorance about other countries, ideally by dropping in little confusing comparisons. "Mt Fuji lives in the heart of all Japanese, in much the same way as the Kangaroo embodies the Australian character." Or, "We have a tradition of training cormorants to catch fish… a bit like you British use bulldogs to herd cattle."

He won't even know where to begin in terms of answering.

Finally, remember you are Japanese and can do none of these things. Still, it would be funny.

6
How to Speak "Half-Japanese"

I can understand a smidgen of French. I used to be able to read Latin quite well. My Russian is all forgotten (despite studying it for four years at school). If I had to say what my "third language" is – after my native English and my fairly decent Japanese – I would probably say it is a variety of pidgin Japanese, the version of Japanese which is spoken by people who have been trying to learn it for somewhere between three months and three years. Or who, for whatever reason, never quite got beyond the basics.

It's a small but significant community (more people than read Latin nowadays, I think). They can communicate to a reasonable degree but usually it's not quite "Japanese as we know it". I sometimes hold conversations in this language with foreigners in Japan whose native language is not English. I remember my very first time doing this: meeting a friendly ethnic Japanese in Kawaguchi, Saitama, who told me: "*Watashi no kara kimashita wa Brazil desu.*"

Occasionally, I speak this language with my friend Mark in England when we do not want our conversation to be understood by those around us. He had no classes in Japanese but did his best to learn it when he lived in Tokyo.

Sometimes I am amazed by what he knows, other times I am amazed by what he doesn't know. And I speak it with my old college friend Chris, who valiantly took classes in Japanese despite living a pampered expat lifestyle in Tokyo that meant he didn't need to. I am the only person he can practise his Japanese on – as he has few Japanese friends. Those Japanese he does know speak English well – and can't fathom his odd Japanese anyway.

I find it an interesting language in itself, in just the same way as I like learning the quirks and oddities of regional variations of Japanese.

Certain traits are immediately obvious. English native speakers will often put heavy stresses on certain syllables or keep starting their sentences with "*watashi wa...*" when a Japanese wouldn't ("*Watashi wa watashi no tomodachi no uchi ni ikimasu*").

I wanted to share some observations with readers, especially as you may at some stage come across someone speaking this strange tongue. In fact, I think the number of people who speak Japanese "a bit" is increasing, and is increasing as a proportion of people who study Japanese.

The early speaker of Japanese will probably have a favourite phrase or two which they will overuse. Typically, this is "*daijōbu*" or "*zenzen*" and "*ichiban*". But sometimes it will be something a bit more obscure. I remember an

Argentinian exchange student for whom almost everything he found in Japan and Japanese culture was "*niteiru*" to his own country or variations thereof ("*sukoshi niteiru*" or "*niteinai*").

My personal quirk was "*dochira demo ii desu*", which trips off the tongue somehow (I also knew *doko* and *nan demo ii desu* but preferred *dochira*). People must have thought I was an easy-going sort.

I rather often started any enquiry with "*komatteimasu*" – which stuck in my head from the second chapter of one of those "Speak Japanese in Three Months" type of books. I probably alarmed a few people before they realised I was only asking the way to Ōji-kōen Station.

My tip, once you observe their favoured phrases, is to use it back to them as it facilitates conversation. (They are probably working quite hard mentally to follow you, so using a word they are accustomed to lightens the work.)

Students of Japanese will often learn lists of words in one sitting, or look them up in dictionaries ad hoc. (You have to start somewhere.) But quite often these lists will not reveal the full nuance of every word, and when you can and can't use it. A "rich flavour" is not "*okanemochi no aji*"; a "thick" soup is not "*buatsui*"; an "old" person is not "*furui*" (or not necessarily).

This kind of error requires the listener to work at

guessing what the speaker is trying to say. Context can help and knowledge of the root language of the speaker might enable you to bridge the gap. It might not be easy, but please don't stare blankly at the person or – even worse – stare at the floor and hope they go away. It's awfully discouraging.

Different standards should apply to pidgin Japanese speakers. In particular, I know that Japanese consider the "*oyaji* gag" to be the lowest form of humour (the very expression makes that clear). BUT for a non-native to make a pun in Japanese is a remarkable achievement. I still remember with some bitterness the time I was at the park and my friend said "What's that bird on the pond?" and I replied *brilliantly* "um, *kamo kamo*". I deserved a round of applause, not an accusation of being an *oyaji*.

Think about it: try to come up with a pun in English right now.

Students of Japanese will have gaps in their vocabulary. Sometimes, these will be unbelievable. I managed to spend five months in Japan before I learned the word "*yōfuku*". I remember substituting "*igirisu no kimono*". Naturally, people were confused and asked me if we had *kimono* in England too.

So: don't be too surprised if someone can speak semi-decent sentences but then doesn't know something really basic. I remember talking to a fine gentleman in my halting Japanese over soba noodle at Okayama Station when he stumped me by asking "*Go-kyōdai wa?*" Strangely, I knew "*kyōdai*" meant Kyoto University but not "siblings".

This unevenness can continue for many years. It was three years before I learned the word "*amaeru*" though "*amae*" is clearly a key concept in Japanese society and I had observed it in action many times. And it was *ten years* before an Australian colleague taught me the word "*bujoku*". It came up at a Makiko Tanaka press conference and my friend, an excellent speaker of Japanese, said: "It's funny. I only just learned that word yesterday and it came up today." I then heard that word about five times in the next week. (So it is useful to teach people common new words: they *might* forget but if it comes up in the next week it will stick in their heads forever.)

Conversely, students may have a sort of party trick: something rather sophisticated that they have learned prematurely. This happens because a student wants to appear clever. Or, it might be fairer to say that they want to show their true intelligence rather than just appear stupid as they speak basic Japanese clumsily. They might start to master the massive range of Japanese terms consisting of two syllables repeated (*giri-giri*, *soko-soko*, *bochi-bochi* and so on). More often it is a saying or two, some advanced bits of vocabulary, or just a normal expression used at the right moment. I remember hearing the famous Australian critic, author and Japanophile Clive James (whose Japanese was a bit average) saying that he practised perfecting his intonation for: "*Honto da to ii no ni naaa*" (to say to people when they told him he was good at Japanese).

Among the few clever bits that I learned in my first year were: "*kō itten*", "*kaikaishiki*" and "*kimodameshi*". ("A splash of red", "opening ceremony" and "a test of courage".) You will notice that pidgin Japanese speakers will desperately steer the conversation around to enable them to show off their trick. (I certainly did.)

The point is: don't assume a speaker is very high level just because they know one or two advanced phrases just as you mustn't assume they don't know the language at all if they don't know basic words, like "vegetable".

Which brings me on to a sore subject: sometimes, a student will look something up and come away with an obscure answer. I looked up the word "vegetable" in my dictionary and it said "*o-na*". Obviously, no one uses this anymore (?) or at least no one understood me when I said in England we typically eat "*niku hitotsu to o-na futatsu*". (Obviously, beginners struggle also with counters.) In fact, I remember someone thinking I said we eat "two women" (*onna*).

I noticed how often I was asked about the English weather and so looked up the word "rainy", except it didn't work when I dropped "*uten*" into conversation. I wanted to explain that English first names traditionally derive from saints – a quick look in the dictionary – "*hijiri no namae kara kuru*"… I practised the phrase "*ryūchō ni hanaseru yō ni naritai*" when in fact 99 percent of Japanese would say "*pera pera*" or just "*jōzu ni naritai*".

Try to be a little sympathetic, as the student may have made a considerable effort to look something up and memorise it. It's disappointing to find out it's been a waste of time. I think I practised saying "*suigara-ire kudasai*" about 20 times before I first used it. It was particularly annoying as I knew the words "*hai*" and "*sara*" already.

Just as a student may have some intelligent Japanese up his sleeve, I am sorry to report that he may also possess a surprisingly well developed knowledge of rude slang, particularly relating to sex. I suppose it's human nature that young men will want to learn naughty words when really they ought to be learning to read Sōseki. And I am afraid they will want to show off this knowledge. It is annoying – but possible – that an otherwise normal person will drop the word "*asadachi*" into an otherwise civilised conversation, and then grin to himself proudly as if he has delivered a stylish quip. Please think of it as an equivalent of that stage when a five-year-old boy keeps talking about poo.

I can remember my own foray into this area. I would joke: I like football "*ashi ga hayai kara*" but I am also good at table tennis, adding "*te ga hayai kara*".

Oddly, a native speaker of English may mispronounce loan words for a long time. The words "silver seat" in English are pronounced very differently from the katakana. People may know the word "salaryman" (it has seeped into English) but the pronunciation is far from the Japanese *sarariiman*. The ingrained pronunciation can stick for a while, even as he learns how to pronounce new (non-loan) words correctly.

Non-native speakers will always be "grammatically challenged". Their mistakes vary according to their native language but word order and use of language may be odd. My friend Chris struggled for years with the idea that using the *masu* form is not always the "polite option". ("*Kare wa ikimasu to iimashita*" etc.) For the record, I still confuse active and passive verbs.

The difficult part is knowing when to overlook the error and when to correct. After all, the main point is communication so it is wrong to halt the conversation at every opportunity and say, "You are doing this wrong."

And certainly, it isn't useful to correct a beginner at every turn. I still remember an incident from 1995 when I had learned the expression "*saki ni dōzo*" and one of my Japanese colleagues sucked his teeth for a while and said, "No, it's '*dōzo, saki ni*'." As if what I said wasn't comprehensible. It damaged my confidence that I would *ever* learn the language.

But it is important to correct mistakes, otherwise they become ingrained and the student is trapped endlessly in this half-language.

One time at my friend's house, his wife poured me a glass of mineral water from an enormous upside-down plastic bottle. It was so big I asked her how she got it to the house: "*Todoite morau no?*"

Her reply was perfect: "*Un, todokete morau*", thus answering my question, correcting my mistake without embarrassing me and allowing the conversation to move along without unnecessary delay. I wonder if she knows why I looked at her right then with such a grateful little smile.

7
Joys of Japanese, Part 2

I am always looking for ways to grab people's attention with a few words. Recently, I came up with the idea that the next time someone asks me what it's like to study Japanese I will say, "It's hilarious."

Needless to say, study is very rarely "funny", at least in the conventional sense. And on the whole there is a lot about learning Japanese that is sheer torture.

Did I ever tell you how hard it is to memorise all those compound words consisting of the sounds "*sho*" "*shō*" "*kyo*" "*kō*" and "*kyō*"? (Not forgetting "*so*" "*sō*" "*shū*" and "*jū*".)

I think I had to learn about a hundred in my first year: *kōkyō, kōkō, shūkyō, kōshō, shōkyo, jūsho, kōsō, kyōsō* and ever on. (Public, high school, religion, negotiate, erase, address, high-rise, competition.)

But I think I could make a fairly convincing argument that Japanese is full of amusing surprises, once you know where to look.

There is still a persistent image that the Japanese are very straight-laced people. It amazed me not only how much drinking goes on, but that drinking has its own vocabulary. One drinks "*sake*" of course but one can indulge in certain variations: "*asa-zake*" (morning sake – perhaps as a treat on holiday) or "*mukae-zake*" (also in the morning, but actually as what we call "hair of the dog"). "*Iwai-zake*" (celebratory drinking) is a tidy expression but my personal favourite is "*yake-zake*" (for which there is no exact equivalent expression). I am a veteran of "*yake-zake*", often drinking hard and late in a vile mood after being forced to tortuously rewrite a story until it's too late to go for a sociable beer – but for years I didn't know that there was a word for this in Japanese.

I hope it's not too crude to add another example of this Japanese trick of fine-tuning a word in this way: "*ne-he*" is to-the-point and relevant. There is a real difference between a gratuitous "*he*" and an unconscious "*ne-he*". I make more use (honest!) of the word "*ne-guse*", as my hair forms elaborate and scarcely manageable shapes overnight. (But we do have a rather good equivalent expression in English: "bed head".)

Japanese seem to communicate quite a lot sub-consciously. People are expected to grasp a situation even when it is not explicitly explained. Sometimes foreigners fail to appreciate what is going on: it is a cliché that Western businessmen sometimes go away thinking they have reached a business agreement when in fact they have been told "*maemuki ni kentō shimasu*", which in fact translates as "no".

I was relieved to discover that sometimes Japanese people themselves fail to realise the situation: that one person, or a small number of people, may not grasp what everyone else does. And then I learned that such people may be called "KY" from "*kūki yomenai*". An apt way of putting it.

Learning the names of animals is usually one of the first things you do in studying a new language. Cat, dog, elephant etc. However, learning the names of rarer animals usually comes quite far down the list of essential vocabulary. As if to spice it up, the Japanese have made some very strange names for unusual animals.

A hedgehog is called a "*harinezumi*". It is evocative to call it a "needle mouse" but a hedgehog is not a mouse (or indeed a rodent of any sort). In the same vein, there is the "*araiguma*" or "wash bear" (which is not a bear but a raccoon). Then there is the "*anaguma*" or "hole bear" (also not a bear – a badger).

I first had the experience of seeing a live kingfisher at Senzoku-ike pond in Tokyo. It was a confusing thing for two reasons. The large number of photographers who had gathered told me they were watching for a "*kawasemi*". A "river cicada", I translated in my head. Well, it's not a river but I suppose that but just means "freshwater", I thought. But obviously I was waiting for some sort of exotic, photogenic *insect*. Except that then a brightly coloured *bird* flashed past for a split second.

The second source of confusion for me was that in my life up till that point I had only ever seen a kingfisher in close-up photographs, usually holding a fish its mouth. It had never occurred to me that this was a little minnow of a fish – I just assumed it was something on the scale of a salmon and the bird holding it something the size of an eagle.

The English word "king" implies mastery and authority but I imagined it implied some sort of hefty physical presence too. So I don't know which is more confusing: calling it a "*semi*" (when it's only an insect-*sized* bird) or calling it a "kingfisher", when it may be colourful and fast, but is tiny and couldn't catch one-fiftieth the quantity of fish an average cormorant can.

Just when I thought there would be no more strangely named animals to discover, a colony of beavers appeared in England in 2014, for the first time in centuries. I wanted to tell my Japanese friend and looked up "*umidanuki*" or "sea raccoon dog". Another highly amusing name for a creature that is not a raccoon dog and doesn't live in the sea!

I was thinking this must be a peculiar Japanese thing

when I noticed that the amusing name "*kaba*" ("river horse") is basically the same in English: hippopotamus being derived from the ancient Greek words for "horse" and "river".

There is a whole world of playfulness in the field of katakana loan words. Someone studying English once asked me if I can recommend a "*power-up* dictionary" – an expression that was at once immediately clear but wholly unusual to an English speaker. I like "*image down*", "*charm point*" and "*last spurt*", only the last of which is used in English (and not all that often). I watched out for these interesting adaptations from English and noticed over the years that they were often used on posters and for "campaigns". I can remember a "*stop za idling*" sticker on a delivery truck (it stopped, engine running, for 10 minutes next to the al fresco dining spot where I was eating). Do I remember a "*no more poi-sute*" campaign around my local *shōtengai*, or am I imagining it?

Certainly, I liked to make up my own "campaigns" in this style: the great "*belly down campaign*" of 2005 (a complete failure), the "*no biiru 2 gatsu*" of 2003 (the longest 28 days in history), the "*stop za chanpon shūkan*" of 2010 (achieved with relative ease) and the "*run za Tamagawa event*" of 2014 (which lent a curious gravitas to what I would normally call "going for a jog").

I also often have a "*my boom*". In 2014, I particularly enjoyed having the "*my Oranjeboom boom*".

Oranjeboom was a popular – if somewhat thin-tasting – lager in England in the 1980s. A lot of people my age remember the catchy TV adverts and wonder why it abruptly disappeared from the shelves. So I was delighted to find it retailed as a bargain *happōshu* in Japan, and found myself humming the tune from the 30-year-old advert.

I don't always follow katakana Japanese. "*Onzarokku*" confused me for a while, partly because I never drink spirits and partly because the pronunciation varies from the English. During one whirlwind, jetlagged trip to Japan I wondered what on earth was this word "Abenomics"– which I kept hearing. (The syllable stress is all wrong if it is meant to echo "Reaganomics".) I vaguely thought it must be the latest "mix" released by the über-cool techno DJ Abe. Stand aside, Ken Ishii…

I have particularly enjoyed Japanese when it subverts the image of Japanese people as "straight" and a bit boring. Learning Japanese showed me that the Japanese are as mischievous and humorous as anyone else. I didn't think, for example, that Japanese would even have the idea of "*kui-nige*" let alone a very abbreviated way of combining words to express it. (The Americans have a good way to say this, in British-English we don't.)

Likewise I was surprised that "*gari-ben*" could express irritation at the overly studious (I thought to study was always glorious in Japan).

I was explaining to a Japanese friend that the hairstyle known as a "combover" is commonly called "the Bobby Charlton" in England – to show how inventive and amusing we are. My friend nodded: "We call that the barcode."

In English I think we need a version of the word "*de-modori*", to mean "kids who have gone away to university but return to their parents' place because they cannot find jobs that pay the rent" or "kids who have lived away for a while but come home to live rent-free in order to save for a house they can never afford". (At the moment, we are experimenting with some phrase about a "boomerang generation".)

"*Poi-sute*", which I used above, is a good expression because I somehow think the onomatopoeic "*poi*" captures the casual arrogance of the tosser.

I am not great at recognising and remembering the names of trees (or plants or flowers) in English, let alone in Japanese. The exception is the "*saru-suberi*" – the "monkey slip" tree. Instantly recognizable, wholly memorable, very funny.

But if I had to give awards for words of this type, the silver would go to "*gyaku-gire*" because I can't believe a concept so complex could be captured with such dazzling simplicity. I remember trying ever so hard to explain to a friend the strange way that Americans seem to react angrily and unreasonably the more clearly they are in the wrong… when he revealed this word to me.

And there was the time, years ago, when I was hitchhiking from somewhere in the north of Japan and found myself in the empty spaces of Ibaraki in the truck of a friendly young man and his charming girlfriend. They proposed that we go to karaoke and that this would be free, as she worked at a drive-in karaoke place and her friend could get us an empty cabin away from the main office – as long as no one saw *her*. Eventually, I asked why it was specifically her they mustn't see. "*Zuru-yasumi*," she explained without a trace of embarrassment. I had known "*yasumi*" for years and "*zurui*" for a few weeks, but never heard the two together. But they clicked together with perfect clarity that day. I give it my gold medal for amusing expressions because I couldn't believe a Japanese person would dare to do such a thing, let alone to so nonchalantly "return to the scene of the crime".

Then she asked a question I will always remember: "Do English ever do *zuru-yasumi*?"

I could have "boiled tea in my belly button". (Is that how you put it?)

8
Embarrassing and Strange Situations Relating to My Life in Japan

Once, I hitchhiked across Seto Ōhashi bridge in the truck of a man speaking a thick Kansai dialect. I had trouble understanding where he was going and where he was going to drop me off, except that the word "Kojima" was repeated a lot. The bridge is famous for having been built over several small islands, cleverly taking advantage of existing land masses to diminish the span and decrease the cost of the bridge. So when I was dropped in "Small Island" I couldn't help but wonder if just perhaps my driver had a delivery on one of these islands.

It all seemed "mainlandish" but I wasn't very familiar with islands – and already had experienced some that appeared as small specks on a map but turned out to be quite big when you are actually on them. So there I was trying to hitchhike but not sure if I was still floating in the Inland Sea or just off the main road to Kobe. In the end, I had to step into a small office to enquire. Somewhere, there must be a lady who recalls a foreigner so pathetically lost he came into her office one day to ask: "Excuse me, is this Honshū?"

◆

I rarely take taxis but of the times I have done so, it has

been overwhelmingly in Japan. So when I get out of a taxi I still think I can just walk away and the door will automatically shut by itself.

I learned to mimic whole sentences before I knew what they meant. I heard "*go-jōsha arigatō gozaimasu*" so many times I was able to repeat it with the same sing-song pronunciation that the conductor uses. ("*Hankyū Rokkō DEgozaiMAsu.*") I asked my Japanese friend to translate it and he told me, reasonably enough, that it was "thank you for your custom".

A year later, I was working in a store in London that was popular with Japanese tourists. I would help them as best as I could in my limited Japanese. And see them off with a confident and cheery: "*go-jōsha arigatō gozaimashita!*"

The first time I camped as an adult was in Kyushu. I hadn't thought it through, and didn't bring a torch to read with, any way of cooking or lighting a fire, or anywhere near enough layers of clothes to keep warm. All I really had was the tent. I had no choice but to go to bed at 9pm and then spend the coldest, most boring sleepless night of my life. I lay there fantasizing about a hot bath as the cold seeped deep into my bones.

The next day I booked into the nearest accommodation available: a caravan. But all it had was a shower, and I really wanted a bath. I spent a nice enough day rambling around but I was still thinking about that bath – as if it would exorcise the lingering horror of the night before. In the early evening, I sought out the public bath only to find that it was closed "due to circumstances" (*tsugō ni yori*) – as frustrating an expression as I know in any language. I asked a local but he told me it was the only one in town. Not put off, I went to one of the big hotels nearby and asked to use their bath but they were quite clear: no "*higaeri*", the bath was for staying guests only. Other hotels in the town were the same, the desk told me.

By now, I was really determined. I moved on to the next biggest hotel with a cunning plan. Sure enough, there was a group of red-faced salarymen in yukata returning from dinner or from an izakaya. I slyly ingratiated myself, asking them where they came from, were they enjoying themselves, how was the hotel? They were quite amused to meet a foreigner who spoke Japanese and asked me to join them for a drink. A drink, then a bath, I figured: the hotel won't kick me out if I am with paying guests… But unfortunately, one of my new friends just so happened to ask a member of staff: "We met this young foreigner, is it okay if he comes in with us?"

So out I went.

My last roll of the dice: I went to a small shop and bought some food and a drink and gently asked if there was anywhere to get a bath round here? It was a small town and I thought, 1) Japanese people will always try to help a customer, even if he is just buying a few sandwiches, especially if he seems a bit desperate, and especially if he is a foreigner and 2) it's a small town and they are sure to be the relation / close friend of a nearby *ryokan* owner and could call him and ask him to let me in.

(I know, I *should have* booked a hotel to start with. But I didn't know there was only one *sentō* in town and didn't know it was closed.)

Instead, and I stress this wasn't my idea at all, after some discussion about the guests-only hotel bath, the closed *sentō*, and the cold campsite, the shopkeeper finally said: "I suppose you could use our bath". I accepted the offer with pitiful gratitude and only a little hesitation.

The lady of the shop then took me into the living quarters in the back, gave me a towel, showed me the bathroom and said: "*Dōzo, shower gurai nara…*"

◆

I took the ferry from Wakkanai to Rishiri Island. I liked the idea of being not just in a remote northern town but going somewhere even further away. Then, on arrival, I conceived of a challenge that I fancied would cement my self-declared status as an adventurer: I would rent a bike and complete a circuit of the whole island.

I boldly declared my intent when I asked to rent the bike. (I noticed that the lady in the shop wasn't hugely impressed but I ignored the obvious conclusion that half the people who borrow her bikes must be doing the same.)

The reply was unexpected: "You need five hours to do that and I close in four hours, so I won't lend to you."

So I lied: "Okay, I will just go up the coast for a bit and come back then."

My assumption was that she was factoring in people stopping for a picnic and also being cautious. Japanese estimates always exaggerate how much time you need, to be sure that no unfit, elderly or careless people get stuck in the middle of a national park at night. I decided I could make it round in less than four hours as long as I didn't dawdle.

I looked at the neatly round island on my map and noted a landmark that was one-quarter of the way. If I couldn't make that in less than an hour, I would turn back. It took me 45 minutes – and I congratulated myself on not being cowed into giving up on my challenge. I cycled on, glorying in the natural beauty of the island and loving the quiet road. I paused at the half-way point: just over an hour and a half! Loads of time.

I stopped for a rest, took some pictures, gazed out to sea for a while. I was really, really happy to be in Japan and doing something I would always remember.

When I set off again, I noted a little shakiness in the leg muscles. I was used to cycling regularly but not long distances in one go. Hmm. I began to wonder.

It wasn't long before I realised my even bigger miscalculation. It seems I had completed the first half with a substantial tailwind most of the way and was now facing a steady headwind. I don't remember enjoying much scenery on the journey back – just a salty sea wind in my face as I pushed my tiring legs. (Sometimes, I ride the exercise bikes at the gym and drive myself on with the reminder that I faced worse on Rishiri Island.)

I got back to the shop, ashen-faced, legs shaking like jelly, in 3 hours 52 minutes, a little wiser and a little fitter.

◆

I like to negotiate a bargain. I always have a strategy for getting the best price, even if it doesn't work out.

I will never, for example, express a clear interest in something that I desperately want. Instead, I will handle it with no more than idle curiosity and ask nonchalantly how much it costs, then put it down with similar disinterest even if I think the price is good. That's because there is always a decent chance the vendor will sell it at a lower price than his first one. At any rate, he won't ask for more. So it's worth pretending you're not interested at that price.

I don't think I am a genius at negotiations but I do think I am pretty sharp compared to a lot of Japanese. It must be a cultural thing because many Japanese, especially middle-class city dwellers seem to be too embarrassed to haggle. I have seen people make their first offer with the most they are willing to pay, which is the cardinal sin of bargaining. I have seen people meekly asking for 200 yen off something priced at 8,000.

As a result, I don't think Japanese vendors are as whip-smart as I have experienced in other cultures. They don't need to be. For example, a good vendor should actually reject someone asking for a tiny discount because it means the customer wants to buy and doesn't have the right stuff to bargain. He will usually fold, even if told something as bland as "I'm afraid that's the price". And the vendor can, anyway, always "reluctantly" give way to the customer's request for 200 yen off in the unlikely event he starts to leave the shop.

So I consider myself a real "shrewd 'un" when I am in Japan: able to achieve bargains no one else can.

One day, I saw a brilliant opportunity. I really wanted a ceramic tanuki for my garden and here was a cluttered little antique shop with three: a small one, a medium one and a large one. I would be happy with the small one. So what I would do is ask about the price of the biggest one. Then, surely, when I asked about the middle one it must be cheaper, then finally when I asked about the small one it must be *at least* 2,000 yen cheaper than the first. I would offer 1,000 yen less than that.

I played out the scene in my head: 7,000 for the big one… I would grimace a bit. 5,000 for the medium one. "Still more than I had budgeted," I would cleverly imply by facial expression and word. 4,000 for the small one. "Would you take 3,000?" Done.

The lady explained that the big one was 3,000 yen. Great, I thought, trying desperately not to radiate excitement: the smaller ones are going to be really cheap. The medium one, though, was "also 3,000 yen". Undeterred, I asked about the small one. "This one is a rare one. Look at the quality; that's why it's in the shop window. 7,000 yen."

Taken aback, I told her I would think about it and left. My plan to work the price down had failed.

It was only on the train home later that I remembered that I was quite willing to pay 3,000 yen and could have had the big one or medium one for that price if only I hadn't had such a great negotiating strategy.

◆

Once, when I was visiting small-town Kyushu I "accidentally" talked a local convenience store owner into letting me use the shower in their house.

They assumed I was staying at a campsite, which had no shower facilities, and I didn't bother to correct them.

It's a long story but I was actually staying in a caravan with a functioning shower.

The next day, when I was leaving town, the kindly manager of the caravan park offered to take me to the train station. I boarded his minibus, with the name of the caravan park emblazoned on the side. Just moments later we were stopped at a traffic light outside the shop where I had showered, for what seemed like a very long time.

I sank down as low as I could in my seat and dared not look through that big shop window for fear of seeing them looking back. Surely, they would see me, surely recognise that it was Yamamoto-san's bus from the caravan park and then surely wonder why on earth that foreigner had wanted to use their shower rather than the one in his rented caravan.

I mean, how on earth would I explain that?

◆

My first ever visit to an onsen did not go as planned. It's hard to believe now but I was really nervous. I had not plucked up the nerve to use a communal bath in my whole first year in Japan. Later, back in England, I felt I had bottled out and missed out on an experience. I resolved that if I ever went back to Japan I would take the plunge.

But it wasn't easy. I was not accustomed to being naked in front of other people. I was certainly not accustomed to the idea of making idle chat with strangers while naked, which I understood could occur in public baths. In my experience, foreigners in Japan tend to attract a certain amount of attention so I doubted I would be left in blissful anonymity in a bath. I asked a local gentleman for a recommendation and he kindly told me about a pleasant hotel by Lake Biwa. In fact, he drove me there since it was on his way and then actually walked me inside. Somehow, he was more enthusiastic than me, explaining to the owner that I had come all the way from England! That I had never been to an onsen before! That I had chosen this area because my friend in Kyoto had said it was famous for its waters!

The manageress was flattered and insisted I wasn't to pay anything (actually, my driver was trying to pay for me).

So you can imagine that my nervousness was balanced by a sense of real gratitude to the nice man and the generous host. I felt obliged to have a great experience in return.

Everything was going well at first. I had already studied the etiquette and was slowly learning to relax despite being naked in the presence of other men. But my decision to open the steamed-up window and get a better view of Lake Biwa was rather unfortunate.

As I opened the second floor window, I somehow managed to destabilise the *amido* (net frame) behind and pop it out of its frame. I managed, miraculously, to catch it before it fell but it was balancing precariously. I had no choice but to stand up, knee-deep in the bath, and try to get it back into place. The comically small towel I had been given would not wrap around my waist, though I tried a few times with one hand (the other holding the *amido*).

It took me several minutes and both hands to reattach the *amido*. It was a smallish bath, facing the lake, so there was no way at all the other guests couldn't see me standing a couple of feet away – as naked as the day I was born – between them and the view they were looking at.

I wondered if they thought I had recklessly damaged the window. I wondered if they were more familiar with these net-frame devices than me, and couldn't comprehend why it was taking me so long to slot back in. I wondered if they thought I was some sort of exhibitionist. I wondered if they could sense I was dying of embarrassment. But I simply couldn't repay my hosts by dropping their *amido* ten foot to the ground.

♦

I know you won't believe one person can be so accident prone, but on my second trip to a public bath – a semi-exposed, simple sort of bath facility at the bottom of a popular tourist mountain – a massive bee decided to buzz me.

It was incredibly steamy and very crowded. No one else, I think, could see the bee. All they would have seen was the naked me trying to run away from it, clutching my tiny towel and whimpering nervously. (I have something of a phobia about bees.) It followed me from one corner to the other, then back for perhaps 40 seconds, before eventually leaving via an open window without disturbing anyone else. They all washed in simple silence.

9
Loose Laughter

I sometimes wonder if there has ever been a scientific study into why some people are prone to laugh at times when it is inappropriate to laugh. It has gotten me into a certain amount of trouble over the years and it would be really helpful if someone could find the cause and, perhaps thereby, a cure.

The last time it happened to me was in the hush of a Tokyo museum. I was viewing a collection of woodblock prints with a friend: pictures of Tokyo from that fascinating period after the Meiji Restoration when new ideas and inventions came in a big rush. Probably, I was trying to look intelligent and show off my paltry knowledge of the subject. ("It's interesting to note how men used to combine Western clothing with Japanese clothing in those years" or "You'll notice that the Asakusa pagoda used to be on the right side of Sensō-ji in those days" etc.)

Then my friend said something that caused me to erupt into noisy and embarrassing laughter. The more people looked at me as if I was weird, the worse it got. I tried to prevent the laughter from escaping but that just seemed to force it out of my nose as a strange snorting sound, which made people start to look *away* – the sure sign that people

9 Loose Laughter

think you are unhinged. And that set me off again. It was quite a while before I recovered my composure. What my friend had said was: "Oh look, it's *No Pan* Pepo" It took about half a second for me to see that she was talking about a poster with a picture of the Tokyo Metropolitan Police's mascot "character". Then another half second before the rush of laughter took over. Strangely, I was shaking with laughter before I had time to analyse what it was that I found so funny.

I had known about Pepo for years and like a lot of foreigners in Japan had found him comical. The cute little character always seemed hopelessly inapt as the chosen representative of the police. Surely he should be a harder creature; the unrelenting, perhaps even intimidating, face of the endless war on crime?

Pepo is the classic example of the need for almost every Japanese organisation, company, campaign, region and product to be fronted by a cute character.

Over the years I kept my eyes open for dodgy characters and would snap pictures of the silliest ones. I didn't take much interest in their names but among my favourites were "Clean Elections-kun" (an angry cat-bird? Of course!), the green furry ball that represents a real estate website (because green furry balls have got to live somewhere, right?) and the "Sendai Onigiri-head".

I don't think I was the only foreigner who found this aspect of Japanese culture amusing but I have to say I was also slightly wary of myself. It struck me as a little bit patronising that some small part of me was sort of thinking, "Ha, Japan is full of these ludicrous little characters and only I – and other foreigners – can see how funny they are."

In my professional and private life I have often been in the position of having to argue the case that Japanese are not weird or wired up differently. Sometimes English people would directly ask me, "Aren't Japanese all mad?" I always contested such questions fiercely. "Certain behaviour may seem unusual to outsiders but they make sense in their historical and cultural context," I would answer. Or, "Things that seemed odd to me when I first came to Japan seem quite normal to me now… There's an internal consistency that isn't always clear from outside." And I would subtly or not so subtly encourage the inquisitor to examine his own prejudices that he would ask such a question.

People would, for example, know that Japanese commuters get "pushed" into trains by handlers at train stations and ask why on earth people would accept it. And I would explain (probably over-explain) how such a thing could happen: How very rapid modernisation since the Meiji era saw a huge concentration of business, politics

9 Loose Laughter

and academia occur in Japan's biggest cities; how Japanese tax laws make it logical for companies to pay their workers' train fares and thereby create an economic incentive for commuters to tolerate long commutes; how train fares are considerably lower than in London (which, by the way, is catching up in the overcrowding stakes) so the simple price mechanism means people are more willing to buy a cheap crowded journey; that acclimatization has enabled people to tolerate less personal space etc.

So, if you follow, for many years I considered it an embarrassing contradiction of my own position that I found the characters so amusing and lacked any rational explanation for it.

What happened the moment my friend mentioned "*No Pan* Pepo" was that my eyes were opened to the fact that Japanese themselves were aware of the oddity of their characters. Indeed, they were looking at them with more scrutiny than I was: I had only noticed that Pepo was odd and had a silly name. I now learned that Japanese were asking, "Why hasn't he got any trousers on?" and giving him a witty alliterative nickname.

It was then explained to me that all Japan was absorbed in this drama of the "*yuru-kyara*". So there was even a phrase for this phenomenon. Did this only catch on in the years since I left Japan? Or had I just failed to notice it?

Either way, it was inescapable now. The king of the *yuru-kyara* is of course Kumamon; I see him everywhere. But there is also the challenger Funassyi and a host of others struggling, a bit like pro wrestlers, to create a distinct identity and a "story" to force their way into a crowded field.

I started to see the *yuru-kyara* from another angle. There is a kind of demented genius in their proliferation. A lot of imagination – misplaced, arguably – has gone into designing and naming them (and sometime giving them personality). I wouldn't know where to begin creating a new character; surely everything's already been done. And yet more come. I was amazed to find that Funassyi isn't even the official mascot of Funabashi City, that we don't know who created it and that it has achieved something close to universal recognition in the space of a couple of years.

So if I recall my laughing fit in the museum, I would say in my unscientific view that there must be a mechanism whereby trying not to laugh out loud is in itself a cause of laughter. But also I think I was laughing not just with amusement about the name "*No Pan* Pepo" but also with a sense or relief. I was relieved to realise that Japanese "shared" my view of their funny, ubiquitous "characters" followed by the realisation that actually it was the other way around: I shared the Japanese view.

10
Schoolboy Sentinels

As I was walking by the Tamagawa one day, something I would-normally-find-annoying happened.

Usually, I walk along the path but on this particular day I wanted to be alone with my thoughts and decided to walk along the less used track at the edge of the river. So I experienced a flash of irritation when I realised that a certain Ochiai-kun was interrupting my reflections by walking unnecessarily – even suspiciously – close beside me.

Obviously, it's unavoidable to find yourself shoulder to shoulder with others in crowded places – the streets around Shinjuku Station, for example. But it is a bit weird when it happens in acres of sparsely populated park space.

As I was walking, I had unconsciously noticed that Ochiai-kun had been *standing still* some way ahead of me. So I found it odd that as I approached him, he took a few steps towards me then – just as I went to pass him – he checked and began to walk in the same direction as me for several metres.

On the one hand, it seemed that he was walking alongside me on purpose but at no point had he actually looked at me, so perhaps he was oblivious of my presence and had just randomly decided to ramble a bit in one direction, then ramble back. I was just about to draw this conclusion when something really odd happened: Ochiai-kun stopped in his tracks and Sada-kun began to walk alongside me at exactly the same pace as me. I watched with a strange fascination as his steps matched mine with spooky precision.

I should fill out the picture a bit. The two young men were outfielders in a game of baseball that was (mostly) happening some distance to my right. I assumed their positions so far out were intended to prevent balls from ending up in the river. They were clearly concentrating on the game, so I doubted that they would have been very aware of me as I strolled towards them. Yet their behaviour seemed purposeful: both had taken a couple of steps infield as I approached, thus ensuring I wasn't walking across their view of the game. And both had then "shadowed" me for a total of 20 metres or so. Their backs were always turned towards me, which is why I had plenty of time to observe their names printed on their team shirts.

I began to wonder if something in the course of the game was dictating their odd movements. Was an excruciatingly slow grounder rolling its way towards the outfield which, first Ochiai-kun, then Sada-kun, was tracking? But no. The pitcher was stood on the mound with the ball in his hand and a batter was rocking on his feet in a "getting ready" kind of way.

So I was rather baffled and about to chalk it up as one of life's little mysteries when the behaviour of a third player (let's call him Yamamoto-kun) helped me solve the puzzle. In the excitement I missed his name – please remember this whole episode only lasted about 20 seconds – but he finally gave me the tiny clue that signalled what was happening. As Sada-kun neared him, he looked straight at him and nodded. Sada-kun then stopped following me and moved quickly to return to his original fielding position. Clearly, the nod meant: "I've got him from here". And indeed the last player marshalled me for the few metres left before I was beyond the field of play.

I was amazed to realise what had happened: the three boys had formed a human barrier to protect me in the very unlikely event of a mighty belt sending the ball flying towards me. At no point had any of them looked directly at me or in any way "shown" me that they were doing me a favour but nonetheless they had worked cooperatively and silently to ensure my safe passage across their patch of the park. During that short period, they had left what were their optimal fielding positions and prioritised my safety. And it had all happened so quickly I hadn't even thanked them.

Now, it may be that the boys' coach has drilled this behaviour into them with threats of punishment. It may even be that a pedestrian had a nasty clunk on the head before this practise was introduced. But it was still a nice thing to experience. Teenagers around the world are generally the terror of their societies: noted for their total lack of concern for others, failing to do anything that's asked of them and generally behaving in anti-social and annoying behaviour. Yet here were three high school students diligently looking after someone who almost didn't realise what they were doing. And I wondered how many people make that same walk and don't realise that unsung sentinels are looking out for them. And then I felt a little ashamed to think that my initial reaction had been one of annoyance.

So I just wanted to say thank you, and sorry, Ochiai-kun, Sada-kun and "Yamamoto-kun". I see what you did there.

11
A Tale of Two Activities

I have a favourite anecdote – stop me if you've heard this one before – about how a sports editor at a British newspaper explained the priorities of his readers. The British are interested in two sports: first there's football and, after that, the rest. In other words, nothing is remotely as popular as football.

In this I am typically British. I will watch rugby if it's on TV. I quite often go to the sumo in Ryōgoku. I try to catch the Oxford-Cambridge Boat Race, or at least find out the result. I have even been to baseball a few times. But it is utterly overwhelmingly football that concerns me.

So it follows that I have taken an interest in Japanese football since I came to Japan. By happy coincidence, the J-League was born within a few months of my arrival in the country, as a student in Kobe. By an even greater stroke of good fortune – for which I owe several people my thanks – I was permitted to "attend" the office of Gamba Osaka as an intern in the weeks around the grand launch. ("Work" wouldn't be the right word here.) Of course, I was an eager Gamba fan.

A few years later, I was living and working in Urawa – a city with a passionate footballing tradition of its own.

Naturally, I became a Reds fan.

In the years since, I have at various stages followed: Shimizu S-Pulse (for a few months, as a reporter, when their English coach Steve Perryman made them the most interesting "story" in Japanese football); FC Tokyo (for the season when they played at the National Stadium and I could easily pop over to watch them after work or between the gym and some drinks in Shinjuku); Yokohama F. Marinos (briefly, because I thought it was cool to go to the stadium where the World Cup final was held); and most recently Kawasaki Frontale (because I have frequently stayed in the area during visits to Japan).

I grew to care for each team. I knew their strengths and weaknesses, had favourite players, learned the chants. But deep down I knew I was doing something profoundly wrong: you can never switch allegiance in football. In normal football terms, if I was a Gamba fan (and I really was) I had to stay a Gamba fan even if I lived in Kanto, even if I could only make it to one or two games a year. If I cared for Urawa (and I honestly did) I shouldn't have been heartbroken when they snatched a late equaliser against Frontale.

In England I have been a fan of Arsenal since I was a boy. I chose them because at the time they happened to have a lot of Irish players (so I thought they were "my" team, as someone of Irish descent). Later, they were a dour defensive team and I loved their grim, British refusal to lose. Miraculously, they were transformed into a flair team with a high concentration of skilful foreign players – and I loved how they stylishly strode to silverware. Latterly, Arsenal struggled to compete as rival teams acquired billionaire sugar daddies and I loved Arsenal for remaining clean and resisting this form of "financial doping".

In other words, Arsenal changed but my commitment to Arsenal never changed, it just adapted to new circumstances.

But somehow I found it was different in Japan; I could change allegiance. Perhaps the reason is that I don't so much care for a particular J-League team as much as care for the J-League and Japanese football.

There's a lot to admire in Japanese football. Firstly, the fans. J-League games don't always sell out. Some are pretty sparsely attended, in fact. But the fans are among the most committed I have seen. I sometimes catch myself watching the fans when I should be watching the game.

Others have written about the "organised" nature of Japanese football fans so I don't think I need to labour the point. But I have noticed, for example, how people at the front wave huge flags when the ball goes out for a corner and – just when I think I am going to miss some of the action – the flags settle down as the player runs up to centre the ball. I enjoy watching the ranks of fans jumping up and down over the course of 90 minutes. Don't they get tired? One hot day I was particularly concerned until I noticed that someone was spraying water over them periodically.

I love the stadiums too. I can hardly bear to think that the old National Stadium is now gone. I spent some wonderful, warm evenings sitting there under the huge sky, beer in hand, while 22 players worked their magic on a beautiful green patch under the spotlights. Newer, roofed stadiums may have their conveniences. I guess they are the future. But I cannot help but feel nostalgic for the older style stadiums, some of which still remain. In 1994, I loved that Banpaku had a cheap standing area behind the goal (the "grassy knoll"). I love that – as I write this 20 years on – it's still terracing.

At Todoroki I only ever go for the "unreserved" ticket; which means I can stand if I want or, if the area isn't packed, can sit on the floor and spread out a bit of a picnic.

English football fans who are old enough to remember bemoan the loss of the terraces where they used to stand. In the 1990s grounds were converted to all-seater stadiums, which coincided with higher prices and a loss of atmosphere. People can stand more densely packed than

11 A Tale of Two Activities

they sit; even choirs stand to sing; people are more animated when standing than when sitting. So it's clear that watching football is an activity best enjoyed upright. Actually, if you look at English fans during big games or during the most exciting moments in any game you will find people on their feet. The seats become just an obstruction.

I wouldn't, however, normally recommend you look too closely at English football fans. It is among the ugliest sights imaginable. Red-faced angry men make obscene gestures and shout vulgar things (you don't need to be an accomplished lip-reader to guess what). They throw coins and other objects at opposition players, or jeer when they are injured. Lots of chants are vile (the word "hate" is very casually used). Some chants are so offensive that they don't bear repeating. At times, I despair at the level of tribal hostility football in England arouses.

At Japanese football games I have heard a bit of booing. I noticed for the first time recently that opposition fans are asked not to go into the home fans sections. But the problems are on a different scale. Would I take a 10-year-old kid to an English football game? Never. Would I take him/her to a J-League game? Definitely.

And in fact lots of children attend J-League games. It's family entertainment. The J-League teams have clearly worked to cultivate the next generation of fans, with a festival atmosphere and events in and around the stadiums as well as cheap tickets for children. Sometimes the kids are just running around the stadium, not watching. I have even seen babies too small to have any idea where they are. Which is all fine; they are being reared as football fans by osmosis. English football has become so expensive that normal families cannot afford to attend regularly. A kid might go as an occasional treat but the ticket costs so much his Dad will make sure he watches properly (when in fact he might not really be ready).

The Japanese teams have worked hard to become part of their local communities. (A round of applause for the J-League founders: that commitment is right there in the founding principles.) It's a story of hubris worthy of a Greek drama that one particular team decided it was above all that: that it could take for granted the support of its home fans, that it could play half its games in another city, that it would be the default team of the whole country, that it could be named after its sponsor not its "hometown"… (And now look where you are!)

I like the players. I haven't seen a Japanese player I would label "lazy" in the way that certain players in England have disgusted me. (Football pitches, by the way, are an exception to my rule that laziness has its place in life.) Japanese players have an excellent work ethic and are generally respectful. I don't just mean that they bow to the pitch when they enter, though that is a nice touch. They are respectful to the referee in that they don't constantly surround him, questioning his every decision and furiously imputing his impartiality. They are respectful to the fans, always completing a proper lap of the ground after the game. They are respectful to the game by not tripping over thin air to claim penalties and not time-wasting from the moment they claim the lead. All of these things blight the English game.

Football fans in Britain today shake their heads in disbelief that Celtic once won the European Cup (the first ever British champions) in 1967 with a squad of players born within 20 miles of their home ground. We know it can never happen again, but it's sad to see how far we have come from those ideals. Nowadays, a Premier League team is said to have a British "core" if it has four players from anywhere in the UK; and it isn't rare to see a starting line up with only one or two (or even no) British players. In 2011, Manchester United fielded a team of eleven players from eleven countries (including one Englishman, one Welshman and one Irishman). In 2009, Arsenal played Portsmouth with neither team fielding a single English player.

Talent is no respecter of nationalism but football does lose something when the teams seem to have no connection to their localities or even their countries. Japanese football is at least mostly Japanese.

Recently, I have been struck by the number of English friends – football lovers – who talk of their detestation of football today. They complain about the things I have mostly mentioned above: the very high number of foreign players; the incredible "wages" of the players; how agents are constantly trying to negotiate more lucrative deals or transfers; the mercenary lack of loyalty players show to their clubs; the play-acting and low-level cheating; not just the high ticket prices but the expensive club merchandise and the cost of food and drink in the grounds.

Premier League football can survive all this criticism because increasingly it is a big business. Fans from all over the world come to see the big clubs. Clubs don't need the local fans and don't need to worry about cultivating the loyalty of local kids. Powerful marketing has made the game so popular that many will pay higher prices to see the games.

But there has been something of a backlash. Recently, I read a magazine article in which a Chelsea fan (and journalist) decided he would go and watch non-league football after a "final straw" moment when invited for a fight at a Chelsea game – by a fellow Chelsea fan. Apart from this last fact, his story was very similar to what my cousin told me recently. A lifelong lover of football, a former season ticket holder, he had decided simply to give up watching Premier League football and now works for a tiny non-league club in Essex. He doesn't do it for the money or for the prestige. He does it because he loves the game and can't stand to see what it's turned into at the upper levels.

Both of them talked about football at the grass roots as being a bit like what football *used to be like*. The players weren't millionaires, they seemed to care for the clubs, games weren't ruinously expensive to attend.

Ultimately, I think that is what I have loved about Japanese football. I have felt a sense of loyalty to and community with the clubs I have supported and an untouched affection for the players. Recently, for example, my team lost a game as a result of a comically inept piece of defending by one player. When the goal was conceded the fans began to chant their team's name more loudly, as if to say, "We still love you" or as if to say to each other, "They need us more now." In England, the same error would have likely resulted in at least groaning and a significant amount of criticism: "You're paid 100 grand a week and you defend like my mum!"

But the really strange thing is that even as I resent the state of English football today, I still can't switch off. Supporting Arsenal is hard-wired into me. I don't know how I would fill the hole it left if I stopped. And the level of play is just extraordinary. There are times when, for example, the Arsenal midfield will create a pattern of one touch passing that is just mesmerising. And times when I think before the game that we are going to lose and instead the performance is unrelentingly brilliant and brave and the team achieves a famous victory. In such moments, I forget the everyday stresses of life. Sometimes I have thought that whatever they pay Alexis Sánchez, with his work rate and his sublime genius, he is a bargain.

I don't mean to denigrate Japanese football when I say it rarely comes close to that level.

One particular happy day, I watched Frontale win 4-1 in Kawasaki and that evening watched Arsenal beat Liverpool 4-1 on television in a bar in Shinbashi. Someone asked me whether I didn't get tired watching that much football in one day. Then someone else said she didn't understand how I could watch Frontale when Arsenal are so much better.

Strangely, neither question had occurred to me. I think it's because I didn't think of them as belonging in the same category, any more than reading a newspaper in the

11 A Tale of Two Activities

morning and reading a novel in the evening. The two are significantly different experiences and I had wholly different expectations of them.

So if I can rephrase my much-loved anecdote, I am interested mainly in two sports: English football and Japanese football.

12
Monkey, My Hero

People sometimes ask, "What is your earliest memory?" Unfortunately, I don't remember. Or at least I can't accurately say which of my early memories happened in which order. It might have been the first time I successfully lied to an adult (at playgroup). I also recall feeling very indignant when my mum ordered me to empty the bin into the dustbin outside (that might have been before I started playgroup). But I digress. I wanted to tell you that I do remember my first cultural contact with Japan, very vividly.

Friday was a special day for me. I would rush home from school. I would request grated cheese sandwiches for tea because, as Earl Sandwich intended, it is a form of food that doesn't require your attention to eat. And I would claim my space in front of our television. It was clearly understood in my house that this was my time and no one could argue it was their turn to choose the channel. It was BBC Two, it was 6pm and that meant *Monkey*!

I almost wrote that I "loved" *Monkey* but as I typed it I realised it wouldn't be right to use the past tense. It still has a place in my heart. I bought the entire set of DVDs as soon as they were released. I watch them from time to time

12 Monkey, My Hero

(I make my nephew watch them with me, as a kind of cover story). I have a little grin on my face as I write this.

And it wasn't just me. My classmates and schoolboys all across the UK adored *Monkey*. It was a bond we shared. If you missed an episode, you would be left out in the playground. We would re-enact scenes from the story. We would imitate Monkey's energetic leaps, his bizarre yelps and his cloud-summoning hand and whistle trick. We didn't just watch Monkey; we wanted to *be* him.

I know the programme was called *Saiyūki* in Japan, but to me it will always be *Monkey*. He was the star, the very core of it all. It didn't work without him. You wouldn't call *Princess Mononoke* "Some Trouble in the Forest" or call *Doraemon* "Adventures of a Schoolboy".

It is difficult to pinpoint a single thing that made the *Monkey* series such extraordinary television. It was, rather, the sum of its considerable parts. As a boy, I loved the action and was fascinated by the shape-shifting and unfamiliar monsters. Watching it again as an adult, I am more taken by the interaction between the characters, particularly between Monkey and Pigsy, and Monkey and Tripitaka. There's a lot of bawdy innuendo, too, that I never noticed as a kid.

The opening is among the most memorable in television history: when Monkey bursts from a magic egg on a mountain. The music is simple, powerful and entirely apt. I have occasionally liked a song that was written for a film. Once, I even liked the soundtrack of a film enough to buy the CD (*The Unforgettable Lightness of Being*). So it's incredible that a whole series of songs written especially for a television show is among my most-listened CDs. I put it on when I am feeling a bit low; "Gandhara" never fails to cheer me up. Brilliant, instantly recognisable Godiego. Their music could shift the atmosphere from hectic and violent to melancholic in an instant. I remember the closing credits showing exotic Asian landscapes while playing "Holy and Bright"; it all seemed so impossibly romantic.

The version we saw was dubbed into English spoken with hammy Oriental accents. I think it may be the only programme I have watched which was *enhanced* by the dubbing. When I watch a foreign film I will always choose the subtitles as I think dubbed voices make it sound wrong and look unnatural. *Monkey* is the exception. The accents are a bit daft; if it were released today, some politically correct dullard would probably claim it was offensive. But *Monkey* isn't a faithful po-faced rendition of the Chinese classic. It's irreverent and fun and the silly accents only add to that.

The lip-synching was charmingly imperfect. As Tom

12 Monkey, My Hero

Geoghegan wrote on the BBC website in 2008: "Say the two words 'Monkey Magic' to a man in his late 30s and he'll turn into a child, putting on a funny voice and then moving his lips in exaggerated fashion."

I say *Monkey* was "dubbed" but there was one little bit left as was. When Tripitaka recited the mantra that caused the metal band on Monkey's head to contract, he would emit a strange sound: *Itete, itete, tetetete*. Unknowingly, this was the first bit of Japanese I ever spoke. I would grip my head, pretend to writhe in pain and let the "*tetetete*" roll off my tongue in sympathy whenever the wicked priest punished poor Monkey this way.

Yet *Monkey* was more than just a vehicle for laughs and fights. It carried within it certain morals about the value of truth, goodness and friendship. Children respond to such things and I was no exception. Monkey may have been a supernatural being but his problems were human. He made mistakes. He got (justifiably!) angry with his friends and deserted them. But he would be drawn back to them through his basic sense of decency. Pigsy's monstrous appetites were both comical and horrifying. He was flawed but his flaws are reflections of our flaws. The unlikely gang hung together in a way that stirred my childish heart.

There was much that was mysterious about *Monkey* (and we didn't have Google to find the answers for us).

We debated the following eagerly:

Is it Japanese or Chinese? We knew that interesting stuff came from Japan and not so much from China (my cousin was a big *Gatchaman* fan). But someone had it on good authority that it was a Chinese story. Eventually, I read somewhere that it was a Nippon Television Network production – and I knew that Nippon meant Japan.

Is Tripitaka a boy or a girl? Opinion divided about 50-50 here. We thought it looked like a girl but we also thought we heard the other guys call "him" "he" at times. I knew he was a priest, and I knew that in England only men can be priests but I remember conjecturing that this wasn't necessarily the case with Buddhism… I watched for the name when the credits came up but we had no way of knowing that Masako is a girl's name.

Monkey is a monkey, Pigsy is a pig… but what on earth is Sandy? Some sort of fish? Why has he got tiny skulls as a necklace? (It wasn't until I came to live in Japan that this mystery was resolved: a kappa!)

We debated who had the best weapon. Pigsy's rake was pretty cool (and not a few English boys got into trouble for swinging their dad's rake around when they were supposed to be clearing the garden). But those lucky few who had seen the first episode knew the incredible back story of Monkey's shrinking staff, which is so heavy no one else but he can lift it. Personally, I wanted Monkey's *cloud*. His cotton wool, glowing pink magic cloud, always ready to whisk him away or enable him to battle it out in the skies.

I suspect Mr Sakai and Mr Nishida could be bemused by all the middle-aged Englishmen who write about them and sometimes try and track them down to talk about work they did over 30 years ago. I hope they can get a sense of what it meant to us. We had never seen anything like it. It burst into our consciousness with all the power that Monkey burst from his stone egg. It crossed cultural barriers with barely a blip. We didn't know for example that there was more than one Buddha and we had no idea why fetching some scriptures would restore order to the world. But no matter, the story carried us along anyway.

For me, the real miracle of *Monkey* was that it was being shown at just the time when the Japanese were developing a real image problem. It's horrible to say but in the late 1970s and 1980s the British had a stereotype image of the Japanese as rather soulless corporate drones, living lives of just work and self-sacrifice for their companies and their country. We thought they were humourless, lacking in individuality and, yes, "inscrutable".

But *Monkey* taught me better. The country that produced such a wonder was to me a fascinating place. And the

Japanese themselves were charismatic, mischievous, brave and strong. Or at least their leader was.

13
Don't Talk to Me About...

Karaoke, sushi, anime, manga, judo, Haruki Murakami.

In no particular order, these are some of the words that have caused me considerable consternation in social interactions. All too often, when I am talking to someone and they discover I have lived in Japan I get the response: "I'd love to go to Japan. You see, I am a big fan of _____" (insert word or words here from the list above).

It puts me in a fix because what people want to hear is amazing anecdotes from the magical land of Japan or at least find their passion is – naturally – shared by someone who has lived in the country: "I once ate sushi so fresh that it twitched when I touched it with my chopsticks!" "There's a six month waiting list to visit the Ghibli Museum but it was worth it. Best day of my life!" And so on.

(Anyone keen to bond with foreign Japanophiles take note and polish your anecdotes.)

But my problem is that, when pushed, I would say that, on the whole, marginally or not so marginally, I dislike all of the above.

It's just my personal point of view. I don't expect anyone to share it with me, but if I may try to explain, again in no particular order.

Judo, kendo, karate or indeed any form of martial arts clearly have their benefits. I am sure they are excellent for physical fitness, are an absorbing pastime and may even be of practical use. My problem is how often people who take up a martial art (especially when they are quite new to it) begin to attribute almost religious significance to it. Among the things I have been told by martial arts acolytes are:

"After practise my *ki* is so aligned that as I walk through Shinjuku Station people just melt out of my way."

(I translate this as: after I finish two hours of practising violence I strut so aggressively that people get out of my way.)

"My teacher can alter the distribution of weight in her body so that she can stand with one foot and one shoulder flush to a wall, raise the other foot and not fall over."

(This isn't possible unless the laws of physics have been repealed.)

"Since starting judo I have realised that everybody in England walks in the wrong way."

(The true way is, apparently, shown only to those who enter the *dōjō*.)

"I just did a week's intense training at a temple in the deep countryside. We got up at dawn, ate and then got into practise…" (story continues for about 25 minutes despite none of the listeners being very interested).

I think you can see I mean is that I don't dislike martial arts per se. I dislike people who want to talk about how martial arts has transformed their lives.

I also don't dislike sushi. Indeed, I actively enjoy eating it. The whole subject of food, though, is one that can grate with me. It seems I am seriously out of step with the modern world on this but I would never consider a meal to be the highlight of a trip, I would never use the words "genius", "magician" or "artist" about a chef and I don't want to see a programme or read a book in which we discover about a country and its culture "through the prism of its food".

I do have memories of certain great meals but for me it was all about the occasion: the friends I was with, the jokes we shared, the special achievement we were marking etc. The food would have played a part (more so, the beer) but wouldn't have taken centre stage.

The most I would like to say after a meal is: "That was good". It would bore me rigid if someone wanted to recall all the details of how gently the fish was fricasseed or how beautifully balanced was the basil on the al dente penne.

Of course there is a certain artistry in making a meal and I admire someone who does their job well. But it's not *actually* art, is it? It's weird to make an idol of a chef just because he makes something you enjoyed eating.

Even odder, for me, is when someone gets praise for knowing a lot about food, or for having eaten at great restaurants. People boast of being a "gourmet" which is, in my view, to boast about doing something essentially passive. The bottom line is they are literally consumers.

Everyone eats, most of us three times a day. Everyone prefers food that tastes good over food that doesn't; most of us know the difference. Can we move on?

I have a collection of about 15 anime DVDs. I am told reliably that they are from the cream of the crop. I paid a bit of a premium for them; in my experience anime DVDs cost two to four times as much as regular films. But I felt I had to persevere; it's such a representative Japanese thing that I thought it my duty to try.

It's mostly a mixture of weird and bad. Dialogue seems weak and stilted – as if it didn't matter much because the film is so "visually stunning". The stories are often barely comprehensible, set in a poorly explained otherworld, future or past. We are supposed to accept this because it is "not our world" and that is what makes anime special. In fact, it often just seems like a cop out for a half-imagined place. There's no way such a setting would be acceptable in a novel or even a regular film.

13 Don't Talk to Me About...

Transformation seems to be a big thing. When I imagine a scene from an anime film, it's always of some sort of absurd, lengthy transmogrification that comes out of nowhere in terms of the storyline (yes, *Akira*, I am talking about you but not *only* you). I can't help but think this is just "because we can": the genre of anime demands it, the story is shaped to fit it.

I recently watched *Howl's Moving Castle* for the third time. (I watched it twice in a week when it first came out because I was to interview Diana Wynne Jones, on whose book it was based.) Here's what I thought: Diana Wynne Jones wrote children's books. She wrote good children's books. I admire her (she is even from the same Oxford college as me). But ultimately she wrote children's books. For children. Making one of her books into an anime film doesn't turn it into entertainment for adults.

Ditto almost the entire anime industry output.

Obviously, there is a lot of anime that is aimed at adults (some of it is even pornographic). But that doesn't make it a grown-up genre.

But what really, really frustrates me about anime is that it doesn't have to be that way. There is a line oft used about musicals in Britain: "I don't like musicals but I do like *Cabaret*." It's viewed as the single work of art in the whole genre. And I have to agree.

Regarding the anime genre, I feel the same about *Grave of the Fireflies*: the incredibly real, compelling, unnerving and poignant masterpiece of anime. Nothing else I have seen comes close. It makes the mud monsters and boys-who-are-also-dragons seem all the sillier and more childish.

Manga and anime form two parts of a single culture to me. Accordingly, my views on the two overlap a lot. They both exist in stupendous volume. In a way, I am in awe of how long the stories can keep running. Statistically speaking, it is incredibly unlikely that none of it achieves greatness. Yet that is almost the case. It is mostly ephemeral and mostly for kids.

In my student days, I used to pick up copies of *Shōnen Jump* from the *gomi* and torturously read "*Kochikame*". It had to be *Shōnen Jump* because it was the only one with added hiragana to aid my poor reading skills. I sometimes liked the stories. I even have a favourite one, set in 1950s shitamachi, as the main character remembered his childhood as a fan of the Mainichi Orions. But I mainly remember it because it was from this story I learned that Japanese people say "*ittekimasu*" when they leave the house (somehow, our teacher didn't think to tell us this) and because I learned the term "*ishiatama*" and wrongly assumed a "stone head" meant a dunce rather than stubborn. But again manga isn't high art. It would be infinitely better for the mind to read War and Peace than to read the entire (197 volumes I believe) output of "*Kochikame*".

And – something you can rarely say concerning Tolstoy – less time-consuming.

It has become something of a ritual that annually we await to see if Haruki Murakami has received the Nobel Prize for Literature. I have experienced this while in Japan a few times and I saw on the news how foreign fans of his gather in a café to await the (non) announcement of his anointment. He is a global phenomenon. His novels are the only Japanese ones I have ever seen read by people on trains in England and the US. (I mean this literally. I have not once seen anyone read Sōseki, Ōe or Tanizaki whereas I have seen people reading Murakami on around a dozen occasions.)

And I just don't get it. I was given a copy of *Norwegian Wood* by a friend, who said it would help me understand Japanese society. I found it cloyingly sentimental. But at least it made sense as a story. Other novels are full of magic sheep, lost cats, talking frogs, protagonists who "disappear" or shift into alternative worlds – mostly at enormous length.

I can see Mr Murakami has a certain something and

phenomenal writing stamina. But his huge popularity is inexplicable to me. Perhaps people like illogical stories, laborious writing and unexplained mysteries. I just don't myself.

I'd really love to be able to sing. There are some old Irish songs that I think I could really bring out the nuances of, if only I had the voice for it. But I don't and that is why the world can thank me for never imposing my awful voice on it.

As my friend Taka once put it, knowing that I was a fellow opponent of the whole idea of karaoke: "People who like music don't like karaoke."

I didn't like karaoke the first time I went. My plan was to circulate around the bar and make new acquaintances while others sang but instead we all, as a group, trooped into a special room and shut the door. We were expected to sing at each other and my friends thought I was only feigning reluctance. In the end I had to leave.

I tried it again three years later as a special favour to some people who had been very nice to me; they had picked me up while hitchhiking even though it had already turned dark (it's hard to get a lift after dusk). Tragically, they pleaded with me to sing *Unchained Melody* as used in the film *Ghost*. Even more tragically, I failed to anticipate that this is an exceptionally difficult song to deliver. They were very polite about it.

It took me a long time to pinpoint what it was about karaoke that I disliked. It wasn't just that I wasn't good at it. Recently, it came to me. Many people now, when they go somewhere iconic or see someone famous, don't want to take a picture of it / them. They want a "selfie" showing themselves with the Eiffel Tower or with Benedict Cumberbatch. In other words, it's not the Taj Mahal that's important – it's the fact of ME being next to it that matters. I am at the centre of the universe and other things merely decorate me. At its worst, that is what karaoke is. It's someone claiming centre stage by appropriating the music created and best performed by other people.

We all have personal likes and dislikes. It's a strange coincidence that a few of my dislikes collide with the very things that other non-Japanese cite as the reason they like Japan. Usually, I have to bite my tongue for the sake of courtesy but it's a blessed relief to let go and air my views for once.

14
"Lesser-Known" Japan

So I don't care much for certain famous Japanese inventions. I am not even into Noh or haiku or Go. It may seem I am not greatly interested in mainstream Japanese culture, but there is so much else to like that I don't have much time to dwell on the bits that don't grab me.

Sometimes, I try to tell people about the less well-known bits of Japanese life because I think they can pick up the main bits from others who are better informed and more enthusiastic than me. I could go on for hours but I would like to mention a few of my favourite bits of Japan that the outside world doesn't know much about.

The Greatest Weed
I know: for someone who claims not to be all that interested in food, I write about it quite a lot. Simply, I can't deny that one of the pleasure of life in Japan is its food. I promise I will never write a book about Japanese food but if I did I know what my working title would be: *It's Not Just Sushi*.

Many people in Britain and the US, when they talk about Japanese food, mean sushi. Some of them seem to think that Japanese food = sushi, or perhaps "sushi and some other stuff". (Ramen has begun to make a mark, too, for example.)

Obviously, that sells tempura and tonkatsu seriously short – and other foodstuffs too numerous to list. But I want to talk about *gobō*. I love *gobō*. I had never eaten it before I went to Japan and it is among the small number of things for which I knew the Japanese word first, then looked up the English word years later (it's burdock).

I am not sure I exactly like the taste but I find it curiously addictive. I hesitated to write this last sentence but I was emboldened by the fact that a few times Japanese have said this to me about gyūdon. i.e. they are not sure they like the taste but crave it anyway.

I have eaten *gobō* in various forms: smothered in mayonnaise in *gobō* salad; deep-fried in the form of *gobō* chips; floating in miso, lightly boiled. Occasionally, I would buy a stick of it at the supermarket and would be amazed at how cheap it was. I can remember scraping off the tough outer skin to reveal the gleaming white underneath and my bemusement when a few moments later this had turned a murky brown – and thinking that it needed another layer removed, only for the same to recur.

When I acquired a house in England with a small garden it was my ambition to grow burdock, so I could use it in recipes here. I knew that it does grow in England because it is used, though only in the form of "dandelion and burdock" herbal tea. However, when I looked it up all I could find was advice on how to *get rid of* burdock from your garden. In other words, it was viewed as a particularly vexing weed. I recall that one website listed several measures to combat burdock which ended with the "when all else fails" option of borrowing a goat for a while, because the goat will gnaw it till it is finally eliminated.

So, growing burdock seemed like a dangerous thing for an amateur gardener – especially one who tends to leave the garden to its own devices for months on end. (In fact, I rather feared my neighbours organising a campaign to evict me for introducing burdock and destroying the local ecosystem.)

The result is that, for me, *gobō* remains a special thing that I only eat when I visit Japan. This makes it more of a delicacy than sushi, which I can buy in the local supermarket or at restaurants all across the country.

"Stores of Knowledge"

Shōtengai (local shopping streets) are at the heart of the experience of living in Japan. A diverse, balanced *shōtengai* adds convenience and value to a neighbourhood. They are fun to wander around and contribute to a feeling of community. I have had many pleasant experiences in small, family run stores and have even written about it before.

Recently, I was thinking about them from a different angle: that they are small storehouses of knowledge and information as much as produce.

In Britain over the last decade there has been a recurring complaint from retailers that customers come in, view the merchandise, take advice from the shop assistants and then leave to order things more cheaply from the internet. That is, they use the shop as a showroom for, mostly, Amazon.

It's true that it happens and I do sympathise with the shops. I also, however, can't help but think they brought it on themselves to a degree. I have had plenty of unpleasant shopping experiences with surly staff in Britain. However, I have also had the experience of myself *being* an ill-informed and irritable shop assistant (during a difficult six months while seeking a better job).

Recently, I was complaining about some of the things that have happened to me in shops. Many times I have gone into a shop with a question and the staff have been unable to answer it. Sometimes, I get passed from assistant to senior assistant to manager and still leave with no answer. Shops are often untidy and difficult to navigate. Sometimes you cannot find the prices on items, or the shop has run out of the one size or colour of whatever you want.

One recent incident particularly riled me. I wanted to

buy a jacket for a female friend but didn't know how women's sizes work – actually I was surprised it wasn't the same as for men. Unfortunately, the system isn't Small, Medium, Large etc. So I asked the assistant what would be an average size for a woman, hoping to guess correctly from there. "It depends on the person," she replied, stating the glaringly obvious. I persisted: "If you tell me what is typical I can work it out from that. If I get it wrong I can bring the jacket back but I would prefer to get it right if possible."

But she insisted: "I can't say. It depends on the person."

I told this story to several friends but only later remembered that I had been a similarly useless assistant myself at a clothes store. I recall on my first day being given literally 40 seconds training (despite having tuned up an hour early for orientation). My first customer asked to see the "stoles" but I didn't know what such an item was. (I should admit that my section dealt with the sale almost entirely of stoles and scarves.) I can remember being bossed around by unpleasant customers and thinking, "I'm not paid enough to put up with this" – and then being less than cheerful with other, innocent customers.

I remember, also, telling a famous singer and his friends who happened to come to the shop that "we don't sell swatches", in the belief that a "Swatch" was a brand of watch. They wanted a sample piece of material (or a "swatch") to take away and see if it suits. I had worked in the clothes shop for months without learning this. To his credit, the singer kindly explained and was not at all snooty.

The experience of shopping in Japan is infinitely better and I have come to automatically expect better service in Japan. In fact, I can remember once asking an assistant in a mobile phone shop for directions to the nearest post office. I was shocked that she didn't know. It's absurd but it seems I had such high expectations of Japanese staff that I expected them to know everything. For the record, she told me the way to the nearest police box so I could ask there. So even then, when I asked something wholly unrelated to her work, she was able to give a good answer.

But I digress. The stores in the *shōtengai* are not just places to buy stuff. They are places to consult and get advice. I have got excellent advice from bike shops over the years. I may sound odd but I can remember a superb analysis on the state of my mountain bike circa 2003. I could: get a few basic repairs for under 10,000 yen and expect the bike to last another year to 18 months; do a bigger repair job for three times that price and extend its life significantly; or replace it with a new bike, which might make sense as it was not a very expensive bike to start with. This may sound obvious advice but I was deeply impressed that he put it so clearly and was just as clearly not just trying to get me drop as much money as possible at his shop.

More recently, I entered a pet shop for the first time since I was a kid. I had found a lost, injured turtle (a long way from any water). I felt I had no choice but to try and save him but I was alarmed that I was not easily able to find simple advice on how to look after him. I was catching insects for him to eat but he wasn't biting. So much was clarified with a trip to the pet shop. My turtle was pronounced fine ("*genki*"), after a look at his under-shell; he should be let out of the water for 10 minutes a day; he wouldn't eat insects till he was older; he would like a few stones to clamber onto; and he would eat this turtle food, which cost 210 yen. I would have given the store owner ten times that just for the guidance.

Real, Real Japanese Clothing

God knows it doesn't need any more publicity but there is a certain clothing company in Japan that I have to admire. I try to live thriftily and learned some years ago that I cannot afford to buy cheap things; that it is of no use to buy rubbish things that don't last just because they are cheap. But I also am not the kind to spend lots on luxury items.

My incredibly unoriginal observation is that a popular Japanese brand of clothing manages to achieve low cost and good quality, alongside a certain unflashy stylishness. As I write this I just checked what I am wearing today and note that my socks, trousers and T-shirt all come from this particular shop. That's not an unlikely coincidence. I have, for one, been wearing this pair of trousers all summer. They are linen, so very good for hot weather. I had linen trousers before but wore them sparingly because they cost a lot. These ones didn't (less than 1,000 yen in a sale) so I am comfortable wearing them out.

The same company is the one that convinced me to try thermal underwear. Previously, such garments were something I associated with elderly people or people living in the wilds of northern Canada. I now wear them around my house in the cold months and have reduced the setting on my thermostat by 1 degree. Clothes that pay for themselves in lower gas bills!

I almost resent this company. It is the one that has duped me into becoming a shopper. I don't go into their shops because I need some item. I now go into the shop to see what they have and end up being convinced that I ought to buy something because it is such good value or so well made.

In 2007, the year I left Japan, they launched an

innovative line of T-shirts with designs derived from interesting company logos and such. I think I bought fifteen of them, including having to track down some limited edition ones at a special store in Harajuku. I was under the impression that this was a one-off but in fact more and more came out in the years since I left. Thankfully, I had left by then because I would have ended up trying to have a "complete" set and running out of closet space.

Some of them are a bit aged now but I still wear them. (I am wearing a favourite one right now.)

I am sure any Japanese reading this knows exactly what company I am talking about. So it may seem strange that I am listing it as "lesser-known Japan". However, it is not a brand that is well known in England. It has some presence but – horribly unfairly – lags far behind a pseudo-Japanese brand that you see everywhere in England.

The English prefer to pay five times as much for T-shirts with dreadfully derivative designs made by an English company pretending to be Japanese. They have a ripped-off brand name. They use a silly mixture of nonsense Japanese phrases and Japanese non-words. Some katakana, some hiragana, some kanji (of which some are Japanese, some Chinese, some neither). I walk down the street and see the names of Tokyo, Osaka and Kyoto emblazoned on the chests of young people, who are presumably unaware that the company that made them is from Cheltenham in Gloucestershire, England.

The most maddening thing is that this company has the nerve to plaster the words "real" and "original" all over its products. All I can say is: "No it isn't" and "No you aren't."

Deeper Japanese Manners

That Japanese are polite and well-mannered is not really in dispute. Sometimes people in Japan express concern about falling standards among the young people. But the broader picture is that people from all over the world admire the level of civility that they see in Japan. I write this on a day that I spoke to a friend who has just arrived in Japan for the first time and needed to get somewhere in Tokyo. She wasn't exactly lost but was asking for directions (in English) pointing at a map. Out of curiosity I asked her, "Did anyone try to take you there?" Sure enough, she had been escorted to one train station and later as far as the point from where she could see her destination. I was surprised not one bit because that is exactly what had happened to me when I used to get lost a quarter of a century ago.

But my view is not just that Japanese manners are good,

or even "not falling as much as people fear". Rather, they are even better than I realised.

I hadn't previously observed, though I am told that it was always the case, that rubbish that was put out in a dangerous condition needed to be marked with the words "*kowaremono*". In hiragana, so that even children can read it. When I look at that neat writing, I feel a little sense of gratitude because I myself am sometimes prone to scour the *gomi* for discarded items. (I have found some delightful crockery this way.) The warning is most welcome to me so I can appreciate how glad the collection teams are. In England, people are requested to wrap broken glass and the like in newspaper but there is a sense that once the rubbish is in a black bin liner in the pile it's no longer your problem.

I sometimes run by the Tamagawa and sometimes by the Regents Canal in London. They share a problem in common, that the path is used by pedestrians and runners and by cyclists. In London, it has become something of a problem. Cyclists tend to travel at high speeds (many people commute along this path). Pedestrians tend to meander, suddenly veering from one side to the other with no apparent logic and with no warning. Sometimes, a cyclist rings his bell – and the pedestrian jumps out of his skin and yells at the "aggressive" cyclist who he thinks is demanding right of way by his annoying use of the bell.

The system is barely functioning. Cyclists do not want to come to a dead stop to accommodate pedestrians who are acting in an oblivious manner. Pedestrians don't want to be bossed around by cyclists who whizz past them at top speed.

At the Tamagawa, I saw the potential answer. Regular cyclists variously slow down, stop or weave around pedestrians. But serious cyclists have placed a sort of "cow bell" on their bikes. This emits a constant but low level sound. Not enough to alarm anyone but clear enough to alert people, via the Doppler Effect, that something is approaching them from behind and at what speed.

It isn't 100 percent. There are still some people wearing headphones, the hard-of-hearing, children and those who apparently think that only things they can see in front of them exist. But it does show a clear attempt to alleviate a problem in a pragmatic and non-confrontational way.

Recently, I bought a pair of shorts and the shop assistant put them in a plastic bag, then closed the top of the bag with a bit of tape. When I got home I noticed that the tape was doubled back on itself at one end, so that it formed a sort of tag. So instead of having to pick at the edge of the tape to get some purchase to tear it off, all I had to do was pull the tag. That's what they call "attention to detail".

The Seed of Wisdom

A long time ago an origami fanatic told me that an American prison had introduced origami classes and that this had significantly improved the behaviour of the inmates because it served as a form of occupational therapy.

I have never been able to ascertain the truth of his claim but it strikes me as entirely possible. I know that use of the hands has a calming effect on certain people and have heard of patients with depressive illnesses in Britain being told, as a first step, to keep busy by washing dishes or anything that uses the hands, concentrates the mind and leads to a desirable result.

A few years ago, I developed my own version of this. I have trouble relaxing and I often have my best thoughts when I am not solely engaged in the act of thinking. I have never, for example, had a good idea for a story while sat in front of a blank document on my computer screen. I sometimes have an excellent idea while out running – and then want to sprint home and write it down before I forget.

I collect *ginnan* (ginkgo nuts).

I am clumsy and impatient and would be wholly unsuited to origami – I would only regret spending money (even a little) on something I inevitably gave up a few weeks later. *Ginnan* gathering is my chosen form of occupational therapy. It gets me out of the house on those days when I lack inspiration for writing or the energy to run.

Occasionally I meet someone else collecting *ginnan* but more often people approach me and ask me what I am doing, or sometimes to give me tips. So it is quite a social thing to do and many of the tips below come from people I met. It seems to me that a lot of people know how to do it but most of them don't do it themselves. So it may be something of a dying art. This doesn't surprise me because I believe it is the most work for the smallest reward of any hunter-gatherer pursuit.

In England, I pick berries but this is relatively straightforward. Wear long sleeves to avoid prickles, pick the ripe fruit, wash it, eat.

Ginnan are an altogether busier business. You don't pick them, you wait for them to fall (in the autumn months) and gather them. One of my "*ginnan* friends" is a retired man who practises pitching and he sometimes throws his baseball at a thick branch to elicit a shower of *ginnan* for me, but this isn't really necessary. Usually, there are hundreds of nuts and no one to collect them.

That probably has a lot to do with the smell. People describe this smell as similar to one of three things: dog mess, vomit or rotten cheese. When I heard the other two explanations I understood what they meant but I had always thought instinctively only of dog mess. Whichever way, the stuff smells unpleasant. You must deliberately head into a place that smells bad and, logically, the stronger the smell the better the crop.

So first you must extract the seed from this stinky, fleshy fruit. There is a technique of gently stepping on them which may result in the seed popping out nicely. It works most of the time, but you still usually get a bit of the sticky orange mess on the seed.

You would be unwise to touch *ginnan* directly, as the flesh can cause a terrible allergic reaction. If you are one of the unfortunate ones, the itching will reportedly drive you mad so it is wisest not to test your luck and to wear gloves (disposable or easy to wash).

You can collect a hundred or two hundred *ginnan* in a relatively short time if you can find a good group of trees. I have a favourite tree but it is near a children's playground so a lot of nuts get squashed by bikes and feet. Not far away is a very prolific tree but its nuts are smaller and the fruit rather stubbornly sticky. Not far away is a tree that drops its nuts a little later so I can continue to harvest for months.

Normally, there are two ways to clean the remaining gunk off the nuts: put them into a string bag and anchor them securely in a running stream; or bury them until the flesh rots off. However, I tend to do this manually by placing them into a bucket with a little water and swirling them vigorously one direction then the other until they are like polished gems.

They dry best in direct sunlight, spread evenly over newspaper. When dry, they can be wrapped in packets of twenty or so in a clean sheet of newspaper, as this allows them to breathe better than plastic bags. If you have a lot, you can refrigerate some but they will lose a bit of their moisture and flavour.

Sometimes, a friend asks me what I have been up to all day and I hesitate to tell him that, mostly, I was collecting nuts. If I do, I usually try to distract him with my two nuggets of information about *ginnan*: that the ginkgo is the official tree of Tokyo and the symbol of Tokyo Metropolitan Government looks just like a gingko leaf. And that the tree is a "living fossil" (a species that closely resembles one known from fossils many millions of years old, with no close relatives). This way, I may bamboozle my friend into thinking I was conducting some sort of palaeontological research or partaking in a cultural experience.

The best way to eat *ginnan* is to gently crack the shell with a nutcracker and then microwave them for 20 seconds.

Add a little salt and you have a perfect beer snack. They also go very well in oatmeal – even the ones that are past their best – and I will often still be eating this in spring.

But you should not wolf down dozens of them in one sitting as, apparently, they contain a minute quantity of a toxin which can cause ill effects if consumed in large amounts.

So by now you must have some idea of how much time and effort goes into getting a few little nuts. It clearly isn't really worth it, on a purely rational analysis. You could buy them at the shop for a few hundred yen and your time would be more efficiently spent doing remunerative work.

Obviously, my point is that I find it enjoyable in itself. Such activities take your mind of everyday irritations and even the bigger, complicated questions of life. During my *ginnan* forays, I sometimes find a solution for some problem I have fretted about for ages. It can come to me quite easily as if my faculties have been freed up. Quite often, a good idea for something to write pops into my head which is why I want to dedicate this short piece to the humble *ginnan*: the most troublesome, most therapeutic and most inspiring little morsel in the world.

15
Strange, Unusual, Rare?

It started badly with the man in the izakaya. Or at least as bad as something can start when someone has just bought me a drink.

He was drinking *nigori-zake* and was determined that I should try it. I explained that I had drunk it on a few occasions and that I didn't hate it but it wasn't my cup of tea. "I'll buy one for you. Just give it a try," he said.

I expanded: "I drank quite a lot of it on a trip to Niigata once. I had a nasty headache the next day and although that was my fault for drinking too much, the taste has unpleasant associations for me."

But by then he was asking the master loudly to pour me a glass on his tab. It was quite a cosy place and several people looked around to witness the spectacle of the foreigner experiencing his "first" taste of something very Japanese. I sipped it with a bit of a sinking heart: surely now there would be great interest in what I thought of it. There would be elation if I liked it; amusement if I hated it and bound to be disappointment if I said that it tasted okay but I preferred to stick to beer.

Instead, suddenly, things went back to normal. The people who were watching turned back to each other and the man who bought me the drink engaged me in polite conversation. I had feared being asked to eat squid guts and horse sashimi but instead found he was interested in the Scottish independence referendum, the differences between the countries of the UK and some of the issues in Britain that have interested me recently.

Then he asked me a question that he must have been itching to ask: "Are the Japanese strange?" I answered, as I usually do, that certain things did seem strange at first but on the whole I was well used to Japan. That certainly some things were different in Japan but that things differ between nations and cultures and, in my view Japan, was not *uniquely* different. I don't think there is an international "norm" from which Japan alone among nations strays wildly. And so on.

It was a pretty little answer, I hoped, but I couldn't help but think my new drinking partner looked a little disappointed. It seemed he wanted to hear something from me that he couldn't have perceived himself. I think he would have been amused rather than hurt to hear a long litany of things that I really struggled to comprehend.

So perhaps, for the record, I should set out some of the things that gripped me as odd or still bemuse me.

Japanese make cats into stationmasters. And give residency rights to seals.

15 Strange, Unusual, Rare?

There are quite a lot of cults and odd religious organisations.

Japanese keep telling foreigners that Japan has four seasons. I wonder if it's a sort of in-joke to see our reactions. Perhaps you could vary it a bit: tell us that you have this interesting phenomenon called "gravity" etc.

Mind you, it seems Japanese do put great store by what season it is. It's a nice day – 20 degrees and the sun is shining – but you can't wear a T-shirt out. If you do (as I did) people will make astonished comments all day: "But it's winter!" It will make no difference to explain that it's sunny. You have to wear what is "seasonally appropriate" not "weather-appropriate".

I fought this for a while but it got to be too much trouble.

Train carriages are not designed to match this. When it is genuinely wintry outside and you are wearing thermal underwear and a thick coat and scarf, the train will be heated to a toasty 22 degrees (more if there is extra heat from a carriage-full of people). In summer, when you are in shorts and a thin T-shirt it will be chilled to warehouse levels.

People consider eating the tiniest bit of charred pizza or toast is dangerous. "It causes cancer," they say. People who smoke will tell you this.

At the *sentō*, there is a temperature gauge next to the

bath. There is a red zone to indicate – strangely – that the water is "hot-to-very-hot but not dangerous". Above the red is another matter: you can scald your skin. Quite often, especially soon after opening time, the needle is firmly into the danger zone. But if you try to add cold water some older man is sure to stop you: "You'll make the water lukewarm!" If you (or actually I mean I) argue the case you (I) will be told: "We Japanese like it hot". The "look at the gauge!" argument doesn't work with them. They claim it's a nationality issue.

In England, "bath towel" means "an especially large and thick towel you use when you get your entire body wet in the bath". The towels people have at the *sentō* are about the size of a handkerchief. And about as thin.

I doubt there's any other country where the government has to force companies to force their employees to use their paid leave.

Yet people are allowed to sleep at their desks. (I never did this but I did go out and get a haircut if work was slow. This would be a pretty unwise thing to do at a British workplace as people can't help but notice you have shorter hair than you did at the meeting an hour ago and must have slipped out of the office during working hours.)

The following are not "typical" occurrences but they happened just often enough for me to think of them as a category of their own: Japanese people claiming not to know things that are known by 100 out of 100 Japanese people. Or more probably 1,000 out of 1,000. I don't mean Japanese who are four years old, or who grew up in Bolivia and recently came to Japan. Educated Japanese adults with jobs and normal social skills.

I used the expression "*ame otoko*" and my colleague claimed not to know it. So I explained it and assured her it was standard Japanese. So she conferred with another colleague. "Never heard of it," he said.

I once told a journalist friend, born and raised in Tokyo, an anecdote about how my worst ever oversleep ended with me being woken by the five o'clock chimes. "What are they?" she asked. "You know. The chimes that ring all across every city, town and village in Japan at five…" "You must live near a factory and it's to tell workers the day is over…" "No, it's across every ward, every neighbourhood of Tokyo and absolutely everywhere for that matter. It's to remind children to get home." "No such thing."

My friend Chris met a Japanese man while travelling in Italy and, to show off to the whole group he was dining with, he encouraged the Japanese guy to have some dessert for his "*betsu bara*". Cue bemusement. "Never heard of such a thing," the guy says. So they all thought Chris was only pretending to know Japanese.

Last one, I promise: In my student days, I told a Japanese friend that I had been learning how to count things, including that I knew rabbits were *ichiwa*, *niwa* etc. He corrected me: "*ippiki, nihiki*". I explained that it was an exception and he (my friend the Japanese teacher, that is) informed me I was wrong. As it happened another friend was also there (a graduate of a top university) so we asked her. "*Ippiki, nihiki,*" she concurred.

SERIOUSLY?

Comedy on television seems remarkably primitive. It consists mainly of one man who is a bit thick and one who is a bit violent. The latter hits the former on the head.

I sometimes point out that this formula is pretty dated now and was perfected and never bettered about 80 years ago by Laurel and Hardy. Then, Japanese people ask who Laurel and Hardy are. Which is strange because they are the most successful and famous comedy duo in history. As famous as Charlie Chaplin.

(Greatly to my benefit) Japanese are unusually interested in what foreigners think of them. I haven't observed this in other countries to anywhere near the same extent. I hear there was even a book in which the theme was "jokes from around the world that mention Japan or the Japanese". So I will share one with you that did the rounds among foreigners living in Japan:

Anthropologists made contact with a lost tribe in the Amazon and sent in three experts to study them. After three months, their findings were released. The French expert had produced a detailed report on their cuisine, their love-making habits and their social values. The American expert had written about what goods they produced, what natural resources they had on their land and about the possibilities for trade. And the Japanese expert had written about (drum roll, please) what they think of Japan.

But thinking back to the man in the izakaya, perhaps the "strangest" thing was not that he wanted to know what I thought about Japan, it's that he also wanted to know about current affairs in Britain. He was a manual worker in a shitamachi bar and he was able to converse with me about my country. I seriously doubt there are many people in Britain of any social class who would know, for example, that Japan's security policy was a hot topic right now. They wouldn't just not know what the situation was – they wouldn't know that it was the topic to ask about. It's very unlikely they would know the name of the Japanese prime minister or *any* Japanese post-war prime minister, for that matter.

It may be stereotyping but the average British working man doesn't read serious newspapers, doesn't know much about world affairs and wouldn't be particularly interested in hearing the views of a passing foreigner on any subject.

In that sense, I suppose the Japanese are "strange".

16
Small Change

When you see someone you haven't seen for a while, you are immediately able to notice changes in their appearance and – to a lesser extent – changes in mannerism, behaviour and character. But if you see that person regularly you are very unlikely to notice any incremental changes.

So it is with Japan and me. Sometimes things really jump out at me that local people are now well used to. I experienced something akin to shock, for example, when I saw a shiny new train come along the Ginza Line. I had thought older, somewhat "retro" trains were part of the *soul* of that line.

People are sometimes aware of this special "skill" I have and ask me to tell them all the interesting ways in which their country has been changing. And it puts me on the spot because, on the whole, I don't think Japan has changed enormously. I might mention to them that there are really a lot more foreign tourists. Or I might amuse them by telling them about the time I couldn't find the Toyoko Line at Shibuya ("It used to be overhead, but now it's about a mile underground!") and how it then didn't take me to Sakuragichō anyway.

But it's hardly earth-shattering stuff. The trouble is that

I don't think Japan has changed very much in the years since I last lived here. I am not even sure it has changed radically in the twenty plus years since I first came.

When I was working as a Tokyo correspondent – let's say a decade ago – I tried to mentally sum up Japan's "situation" in a few sentences: Japan has a stagnant economy that only achieves growth through massive public spending and growing public debt. It has an ageing population and a low birth rate. Women are not well represented in society. One party seems always to return to power, however much it appears that a new political era is emerging. Japan doesn't have great relations with its Asian neighbours and is in danger of being overtaken by China.

I could almost have written the same sentences a decade earlier, or today. I think of the *saodake* van that used to drive around my old neighbourhood as a sort of symbol of Japan. You know: "*20 nen mae to onaji…*"

Even the things that I think have changed don't always bear too close scrutiny. I love that an excellent craft beer tradition has developed in the years since I first arrived. But still if you head to an izakaya in Tokyo, it's 90 percent certain it will only serve one type of beer (and it's very likely to be Super Dry).

I love football and admire the progress made by Japanese players since the J-League started. But attendance

16 Small Change

at football games still lags miles behind that of baseball. (How do they fill all those stadiums when it's the same two teams playing every day, time after time?)

Obviously, I am not saying that there has been no change in Japan. Rather that it changes less than people think. People said that Japanese politics would "never be the same" after the 2011 earthquake and tsunami. But isn't this the same Shinzō Abe who was prime minister when I left Japan?

It seems that in the face of disaster, people like to claim some small solace from assuming that things simply cannot carry on as before; that the calamity is given meaning by the changes that flow from it. I am sorry to say that it is not necessarily the case.

When I was a Tokyo correspondent, I yearned for big changes. Big changes were newsworthy. Sometimes, in the absence of actual change, I was asked to anticipate things that "could" happen or were in the pipeline. I can remember, for example, being asked to write about Japan's "steps towards" acquiring nuclear weapons. (I resisted writing the story, to little effect). One of the last pieces I was asked to write for the newspaper, in 2007, was about how Japan was moving towards changing Article Nine of its constitution.

These would have indeed been major changes – if they

had happened.

One of the stories that sat on my "to do one day" list was the plan to bury the expressway that currently runs over Nihonbashi Bridge. I first heard of this plan in 1998, I believe. "That'll make a story when it happens," I thought. I am still waiting.

Even things that seemed like big developments look less dramatic in retrospect. I wonder now why I thought Junichiro Koizumi's "bold" Post Office privatisation to be "big news". In terms of impact on people's lives I now think "cool biz" was more important.

Certainly, my own country seems to have changed a lot more than Japan in the years since I left university. To pick a few examples:

We have become a country with a very large number of immigrants. The number of people in the UK who were born overseas is set to reach eight million; close to double the combined populations of Birmingham, Liverpool, Leeds, Sheffield, Bristol, Manchester, Leicester and Coventry.

Property prices in London have approximately tripled in the space of the last decade, putting even a small apartment out of reach for the majority of young Britons.

Homosexuals can now legally marry and adopt children in Great Britain.

The House of Lords ceased to have hereditary peers.

The United Kingdom is less "united" that it was. Wales and Scotland achieved a high degree of devolution in 1997. In 2014, Scotland almost voted to split away from the UK. Instead, it will now get considerable new powers which will almost certainly lead for calls for more powers for other regions of the country, including demands for the English to have more say over their exclusive affairs.

Northern Ireland has achieved a remarkable level of stability through a complicated and uneasy peace process, which has fundamentally changed the most troubled region of the UK.

I think you can see that the scale of change in the UK makes change in Japan seem less radical.

I am not saying change per se is necessarily good. (I have reservations about many of the changes that have happened in the UK, as you can probably infer.) Indeed, I like that many good things about Japan haven't changed (or have improved): the high degree of social cohesion, the excellent public transport, the relatively low levels of crime etc.

Nor am I saying that Japan is somehow inherently unable to change. The Meiji revolution (I think that's more accurate than "restoration") is one of the great subjects in modern history, as a feudal society was transformed into an advanced nation in a generation. And in the aftermath of World War II, Japan was wholly reborn.

But as far as I can see we are not living in such dramatic times. It may even be a disappointment to some people that when I look at Japan several years after I left it, I notice mostly lots of little things. Here's one: When I first came to Japan, children sometimes saw me and said "*Amerika-jin da*", a few years later it was "*gaijin ga iru*", now for some reason they say "YOU *ga iru*".

17
What I Thought Then, What I Think Now

The ancient Greeks told us you cannot step into the same river twice, meaning that even if you return to a place it will have changed in the meantime. More importantly, you yourself will have changed so even if you think you are doing the same thing you did before you are actually doing it as a different person, with a different experience of life and a different perspective.

That's certainly true of me. My view on many things has changed between the time when I lived in Japan – say 10 years ago – and now. Here are some thoughts on some characteristically Japanese sights.

◆**There are 300 young people leaving some sort of company organised event for new employees (a *nyūsha-shiki* or a *setsumeikai*?) They are all, without exception, boys and girls, wearing black suits and white shirts.**

I thought: Wow, I can see why people think Japanese are very conformist. I am sure each of these people is very individual with their own hobbies and personalities but right now they *look* spookily uniform.

On second thoughts: If you know the other 299 people will be dressed like that, it would *really* need guts to wear a purple shirt.

◆**There is a huge queue for an izakaya. (It's one I tried to go to once and I remember that it closes at 10pm, last order at 9.20pm.)**

I thought: I wonder how many people in that queue are "*sakura*" and how many are people who queue because they see the queue and think it must be worth a visit because it's worth queuing for.

On second thoughts: I believe two of the core principles of economics are profit maximisation and rationing of scarce goods via the price mechanism. So it would seem that Japan is not a proper capitalist economy. If it were, this restaurant would either expand, open a branch nearby to cope with the overflow or extend its opening hours. Or it could just raise its prices.

◆**It's cherry blossom season and the best spots in the park are roped off with no people sitting within. Taped paper signs say the name of the organisation that has "reserved" this area for later.**

I thought: Only in Japan would people respect this system.

On second thoughts: Actually it would just be funny to print and bring your own signs to tape over the top: "Feel free to use this space!"

◆ *Hanami*: a brief, beautiful time of year. Blue sheets everywhere.

I thought: Japanese are really organised about picnicking. The sheets are waterproof, easy to clean etc.

On second thoughts: Blue sheets are really ugly and unnatural. Surely cardboard is infinitely less jarring, disposable and recyclable.

◆ In a restaurant, the staff are bringing some sort of giant fold-out bag to the customers to put their bags into, so they don't have to be placed on the floor.

I thought: Nothing actually – unless I am greatly mistaken this "service" was invented since I left Japan. (Curiously, several people have said to me that this has "always" been done.)

On first impression: I thought bags were to put things into so that the things don't get dirty. Now the bag has to have a bag to go into?

◆ In a shop, the staff are offering baskets to customers who have more than one or two items in their hands.

I thought: Classic Japanese service! The attentive staff are noticing when customers need a hand.

On second thoughts: Very clever indeed! While offering good customer service, they are also increasing the chances that customers will pick up some more items before heading to the till.

◆**The television news is nearly over but there's time for just one more story. It's about primary school children in Mie Prefecture gathering acorns because it's acorn-gathering season. Or schoolchildren in Ehime Prefecture planting rice because it's rice planting season etc.**

I thought: This is the Japanese equivalent of the "cheery" bit of news that we used to have in England for light relief after all the tales of death and destruction. There's a dog in Clapham that can tap dance or there's a farmhouse pig that has adopted a baby kitten abandoned by its mother.

On second thoughts: Sadly, half the working population of Japan sees so little nature that these little news bits are probably the closest they get to experiencing the changing seasons in their daily routines.

◆**It's election time. Vans are driving round and round the neighbourhood, noisily shouting empty slogans and repeating names over and over again. I know they will be hanging around the station and the *shōtengai* "noising it up" too.**

I thought: I am trying to work, or I am trying to relax. I might even be trying to have a nap. I am in my own place. I am paying for this. Yet I have to listen to this noise pollution and I can't do a damn thing about it. I can't even vote against the noisiest candidate. AAAAARRRGGGGHHHH!

On second thoughts: I am trying to work, or I am trying to relax. I might even be trying to have a nap. I am in my own place. I am paying for this. Yet I have to listen to this noise pollution and I can't do a damn thing about it. I can't even vote against the noisiest candidate. AAAAARRRRGGGGHHHH!

◆**The end of the year. There's an enormous line at a booth selling lottery tickets. It looks like at least a 45 minute wait. There is another booth nearby where no one is queuing. But nobody will switch queues because they want to buy from the booth that once sold a super lotto winning ticket.**

I thought: Gamblers are really superstitious. Surely they should see a ticket sold at one booth has exactly the same mathematical odds as one sold at another, regardless of any irrelevant "history".

On second thoughts: Why doesn't anyone seem to be superstitious the other way around? According to my underwhelming maths, if the chance of any one ticket winning the jackpot is a billion to one, then the chances of the same booth selling the winner twice must be 40 trillion to one. i.e., "That booth that has already sold its allotted share of winning tickets for the next 160,000 years. I'd best avoid it".

◆**A bookshop. Lots of people are standing around reading the entire content of books and magazines. There's even a word for this in Japanese (*tachi-yomi*) which has no English equivalent. We say "browsing" to mean "reading a bit of a book to see if we want to buy it".**

I thought: Why are people so tight that they won't shell out for a book they want to read? Don't they know about libraries? Why don't the bookstores chase them away?

On second thoughts: Go on, buy this book. Please. I spent *years* working on it!

18
I Could Fill a Book with the Things I Didn't Know

One of the best pieces of advice I received when starting out in journalism was that "there's no font for irony". I use irony all the time when speaking, so naturally I was tempted to write that way. But, forewarned, I realised that my written words could easily be misinterpreted as sincere. I imagined friends telling me that they saw my tribute to Tony Blair when what I had sarcastically written was: "Blair has really proved himself to be a 'pretty straight sort of guy'". Or getting polite letters of explanation from readers in response to my ironic suggestion that "surely the Japanese government should build some more expressways to boost the economy".

Well, now I would like you to imagine that I am writing in a font that indicates embarrassment. Because that is what I am feeling as I write.

For years, I viewed myself as a "Japan hand". I only feigned reluctance to accept the praise when Japanese people said, "You know more about Japan than we Japanese do!" I barely bothered to deny that I was an expert on Japan when introduced that way to English people. Instead I would just say, "Well, I did live there for 15 years so obviously I got to know the place quite well."

And yet, returning to Japan on trips I found that there were all sorts of things I didn't know at all. Not obscure or rare things, either; things an ordinary Japan resident might reasonably have been expected to know but I had not enquired into or perhaps simply overlooked.

At the risk of looking silly – and please remember the special "embarrassment font" I am using – I decided to make a list of them, which may be of interest to you. I call it: "Things I really ought to have known if I was half as clever as I thought I was."

Firstly, places. I used to say that I had been "all over Japan". I had made a big trip to Hokkaido when I thought I might be leaving Japan in 1997. I had lived in Kobe and Tokyo and had moved around both regions thoroughly. I "did" Kyushu twice, I had a special fondness for Shikoku. I stayed in Hiroshima often, Niigata a couple of times and Nagoya once. I went to Kanazawa, Okayama and Kurashiki; Rishiri Island, Naoshima, Miyakejima and Sakurajima. I had looked at a map and decided, with no real knowledge of the place, to hitchhike to Noto Peninsula and spend a few days there. (I slept in a tent under a sign warning me to beware of being kidnapped to North Korea. It was 1998 and I considered it a local fairytale.) I finally went to Okinawa on a work trip the year before I left Japan. I fancied myself pretty well travelled.

In 2014 and 2015 I decided to seek out the last remaining "obscure" places I had missed. I owe a formal apology to the following places: Aizuwakamatsu, Akita, Hiraizumi, Hirosaki, Matsumoto and Nagano. You were all very interesting and very enjoyable. I could write a decent travelogue on each place. I certainly told friends in Japan why they should visit. But the most appalling fact is that, as of 2013, I had not even heard of three of these places, knew two of them only by name (I couldn't have located them on a map) and the other I knew mainly in the context of a rather grubby news story.

It follows that I had never heard the story of the Byakkotai or the resistance of the Aizu clan to the Meiji Restoration. I may have seen the Namahage in a vintage NHK documentary, but then again that may have been some other demons and some other region. I didn't know that a special stick representing Buddha comes out every seven years at Zenkō-ji. I didn't know that Hiraizumi has a particularly beautiful temple – and, sorry, but I didn't hear of it and decide to go because it achieved World Heritage status. I decided to go almost by accident and found out when I got there that it was celebrating its new status. I didn't know that Matsumoto had one of the few "real" castles left in Japan – and I didn't know that you could have a castle that's five stories from the outside but six on the inside.

I didn't know Nagano Prefecture has bees the size of birds. I didn't know that you should make a lot of noise as you walk through forested mountains, so as to warn bears away. (Coming from England, I didn't imagine that bears were something you might meet. And I might have thought it best to be quiet so they don't hear you and come and eat you. It took me quite a while to realise that the wooden hammer and hanging planks at various intervals along the path were for me to whack loudly.)

My oversights extended to the places I knew best of all. I had wandered and cycled all over Tokyo, or so I thought. Then one day I was taken to Todoroki Ravine Park, which was somewhat otherworldly. You step off a normal Tokyo street and you are in what appears to be an ancient forest.

I also found the Tamagawadai Park, which is a mere 3.5 km from the apartment I lived in for seven years. The odd thing is that this is *exactly* the kind of place I would have wanted to know about. I like parks, I like rivers, I like slightly elevated places and I like anything that has a bit of history. Tamagawadai is a raised park by the Tama River which houses several ancient burial mounds and an exhibition space explaining about the history. I cannot believe that in my many wanderings I never found it.

I could bore you with the long list of words that I

managed to live without for fifteen years but now hear all the time. But I will stick to a couple that particularly amaze me. I only learned there's a fish called *hata hata* a few months ago, which is odd because I spent a lot of time eating fish in Japan. And "the peppery flakes that you put on yakitori" is called *shichimi* (literally "seven flavours", so not exactly hard to learn or hard to memorise). I stress that I didn't forget these words. I didn't know them in the first place.

I had never seen the vegetable *kogomi*. When I "discovered" it at a small grocer in Aomori, I thought it was a rare local delicacy and brought it back as cheap *omiyage* for a friend. I subsequently found it at my local grocer, and grocers all over the place, and eat it all the time. (I don't particularly like green vegetables so the mild taste of this one suits me nicely.)

Then a few days later I discovered *komatsuna*.

You know how there's *kitsune udon* and *tanuki udon*, but they aren't made using foxes or raccoon dogs? I concluded that noodle-based dishes are often given animal nicknames. So it followed that there was such a thing as "monkey soba". i.e. I assumed the "*zaru*" of *zaru soba* was the same "*zaru*" as in "*yamazaru*". I only learned recently, by sheer chance, that this was wrong.

Somehow, Hibari Misora passed me by despite being

ranked number six in a newspaper poll of which people represent post-war Japan. I subsequently found her most famous song "*Kawa no nagare no yō ni*" on YouTube and can say it's wholly unfamiliar to me.

Incidentally, the other 19 people in the list were all men. So I must conclude that post-war Japanese society has a strong gender bias. But I must be even more sexist as I knew all the 19 men and not the lone woman.

I must have seen cedar balls hanging outside shops at some point in my Japan years. Why was I not curious about them? Did I just assume they were some sort of decoration? Now, of course, I know they are there to indicate "new sake is ready"; an attractive and natural form of advertisement.

Nor did it occur to me that there was a brewing season, until I turned up to ask for a tour of a sake brewer in Hachinohe – during the off-season. They gave me a very informative personal tour anyway. (Thanks, guys.) I now know that the god of sake is a female divinity and her "jealousy" is why women didn't used to work in sake production.

Not everyone likes graveyards but I think they are often beautifully maintained places with real character. I have visited many all across Japan but do not recall ever noticing the *gorintō* style of grave, which is now my "favourite".

They are among the few structures that become more interesting and attractive as they age, which makes sense as they are intended to be around for a long time. Obviously, I did not also know that the five stones represent the five elements. Actually, I didn't know that there were five elements in Buddhist thought, let alone what they were.

It's not just that I lived in Japan a long time. As a journalist, it was my role to understand and explain things. I prided myself on my inquisitive nature and thought I was doing rather well. I even felt confident enough to write a book on Japan. So it's an embarrassment tinged with shame to discover how much I was missing. It's not much of an excuse but I think people get trapped into routines and stop noticing new things. If I had a spare afternoon, I went to Senzoku-ike Park. I liked it and it was five minutes away so I didn't need to find another park. If I had a three day break, I went to Shimoda. I always enjoyed it and it was cheaper to get there and back than Matsumoto. I went to Ikegami Honmon-ji 20 times and never to Gokoku-ji. (I corrected that recently.) It took being away from Japan to jolt me out of my lifestyle.

I came to Japan for *hanami* one year and I was somewhat perturbed to hear that Somei Yoshino trees don't seed; that they are grown from saplings from another tree. So that's why they all blossom at almost the exact same time as nearby trees. In effect, they are clones that have spread across Japan and even into Washington DC. It made me yearn for a bit more "natural nature", hybrid vigour and diversity.

To rush through a few things I hadn't known. I didn't know about "*michi no eki*". I have come to rather like them as a sort of museum of local produce to browse. I learned that the era during which all those "*kofun*" (burial mounds) were made is called, appropriately enough, the Kofun period. I learned about the Jōmon period, including why it's called that. I learned that Sannai Maruyama in Aomori was possibly the "capital" of Japan in its heyday four and a half thousand years ago.

Dogū are historical carvings, but also cute and attractive. They are the only kind of Japanese "character" that I want to have hanging in my house.

I can now see that not all the stone walls on castles are equally impenetrable: there is clear evolution as big rocks with gaps gave way to more regular slabs of rocks and finally smooth-faced rocks with sharp inclines. (I also now know the word "*musha-gaeshi*".)

The main thing that I have learned about Japan is that it is even more interesting than I realised. There are more places to visit. There are fascinating aspects of Japanese culture that I hadn't noticed. There are ideas, words and sights that I hadn't known about.

Thank heavens I now know everything there is to know about Japan and can relax, safe in my great wisdom.

(And yes, that last sentence is ironic.)

Afterword

Ten years ago, when I was invited to write a book about my experience of Japan, I was sure of one thing: I would never get a chance like it again. So I crammed in as much as I could of what I learned, what I loved and what I felt about Japan from my time living there. I held nothing back.

So it was with some trepidation that I turned towards writing this book. Fortunately, I had quite a bit of time to work on it and a lot of help. But most importantly I had a good subject: Japan and its people.

Living away from Japan made me look at it in a new light. I remembered many things that I had forgotten. I noted what stories my British and American friend seemed to be interested in – and they weren't always the stories I thought were most interesting. When I returned, I noticed many new things, some of which were new but some of which were just new to me.

In the end, this was quite an easy book to write. I spent time in Japan observing and making notes, but the material was basically there in front of me.

In this book I don't try to analyse Japan's political system, its society or culture in any rigorous or in-depth way. I hope no one was fooled by the "textbook" title; like much else in the book, it isn't meant to be taken too seriously. My approach is rather scattershot and it's a quite personal book in that it's basically what I wanted to write about, written how I wanted to write it. So its many shortcomings are a reflection of my shortcomings.

I gathered ideas for this book during several visits to Japan, some of them lengthy. I am really grateful to the numerous people who hosted me, helped me enjoy those times so much and nudged me towards new experiences.

This book couldn't have happened without the help and advice of Shiro Hayashi and everyone at Sankensha. Hiroyuki Morita has been endlessly patient and encouraging. They are more than "great people to work with", they are great people.

Chris Barton has always generous with his friendship, hospitality and advice, including during work on this book.

I am grateful to Takeshi Nakano of NHK Publishing who supervised my first book in English and never once complained about all the trouble I caused him.

I didn't have the good fortune to meet Mr Hiroyuki Tanaka, who supervised sales of my first book at NHK Publishing, before his untimely death. But it was an honour to have such a diligent young man in my corner.

Lastly, I want to say to all those readers who kindly bought this book – and especially those who read it carefully – *go-jōsha arigatō gozaimashita*!

Profile

Colin Joyce was born in 1970 in Romford, Essex, though due to a mix-up his passport says he is from Dagenham (one of the few places in England less fashionable than Romford).

He was encouraged by his history teachers to try for university and – driven on by a burning desire to live in a town with a bookshop – he secured a place at Oxford. He even won a scholarship of £100 a year, which may not sound like much but beer was 60 pence a pint in the college bar back then.

After graduating with a degree in Ancient and Modern History, he went to Kobe with the aim of mastering Japanese in nine months. It took him nine days to realise he would need about nine years.

He endured a spell as an incompetent shop assistant (in London) and an even worse teacher at a prefectural high

school (in Saitama) before trying his hand at journalism, because he wanted to make people pay attention to him.

He worked as an editor and reporter for *Newsweek Japan* magazine and then as Tokyo correspondent for the UK national newspaper, *The Daily Telegraph*. His book *How to Japan* was based on his experiences living and working in Japan for a total of 15 years.

A three-year stay in the US (which inspired another book, *An Englishman in N.Y.*) was followed by a return to Britain in 2010 where he discovered that a lot of things had changed in his absence. Notably, house prices had risen so much that not only couldn't he afford to live in London, he couldn't even afford to move back to Romford.

His book *Let's England* is partly about his "culture shock" at finding his country had the temerity to change when he was only away for a couple of decades. A collection of essays, *London Calling*, is also available in book format with text in both English and Japanese.

He is of Irish descent so it's not impossible that he is incredibly distantly related to James Joyce, which may explain why – despite a shared literary genius – their literary styles differ somewhat.

He currently lives in Colchester, which he proudly refers to as "the most cultural place in Essex".

Now How to Japan
Fresh Discoveries, Further Reflections

2016年4月15日　第1刷発行

著者　　コリン・ジョイス
　　　　© 2016 Colin Joyce
発行者　林 良二
発行所　株式会社 三賢社
　　　　〒113-0021　東京都文京区本駒込4-27-2
　　　　電話　03-3824-6422
　　　　FAX　03-3824-6410
　　　　URL　http://www.sankenbook.co.jp

印刷・製本　中央精版印刷株式会社

本書の無断複製・転載を禁じます。落丁・乱丁本はお取り替えいたします。定価はカバーに表示してあります。

Printed in Japan
ISBN978-4-908655-01-2 C0082

ブックデザイン　　佐藤裕久
　　編集協力　　森田浩之